Y0-AVB-005

SEX IN THE BIBLE

TOM HORNER

CHARLES E. TUTTLE COMPANY
Rutland • Vermont Tokyo • Japan

Representatives

For Continental Europe:
BOXERBOOKS, INC., *Zurich*

For the British Isles:
PRENTICE-HALL INTERNATIONAL, INC., *London*

For Australasia:
PAUL FLESCH & CO., PTY. LTD., *Melbourne*

For Canada:
M. G. HURTIG PUBLISHERS, *Edmonton*

Published by the Charles E. Tuttle Company, Inc.
of Rutland, Vermont & Tokyo, Japan
with editorial offices at
Suido 1-chome 2-6 Bunkyo-ku, Tokyo

Library of Congress Catalog Card No. 73–87676
International Standard Book No. 0–8048 1124–5

First printing, 1974

Printed in Japau

This book is dedicated
to all those I taught
at the
Philadelphia Divinity School
1957–69

TABLE OF CONTENTS

ACKNOWLEDGMENTS

THE SCRIPTURE quotations in this publication (unless otherwise noted) are from the *Revised Standard Version of the Bible,* copyrighted 1946 and 1952 by the Division of Christian Education of the National Council of the Churches of Christ in the U.S.A., and used by permission.

Quotations from *Encyclopaedia Britannica,* © 1962, reprinted by permission.

For permission to quote copyrighted material the author would also like to thank the following:

G. & C. Merriam Company, Springfield, Massachusetts, for permission to quote from *Webster's Seventh New Collegiate Dictionary,* 1971.

Penguin Books, Ltd., for permission to quote from *Herodotus: The Histories,* translated by Aubrey de Sélincourt, © The Estate of Aubrey de Sélincourt, 1954.

* * *

In the *Revised Standard Version of the Bible,* the word LORD indicates the presence of the divine name YAHWEH in the original Hebrew text of the Old Testament. The *King James Version* had earlier followed this same practice.

PREFACE

WITHOUT DOUBT the Bible has been the most influential book in Western civilization—and also one of the most misunderstood. The misunderstanding will continue until people change their attitudes. To begin with they must realize that the Bible is a very human book.

The public is not entirely to blame in this matter of Biblical ignorance. Churches and teachers of religion have fostered the condition somewhat. If a passage is the least bit spicy, or if it offends in any way, they have deleted it from their Sunday School lessons, from their sermons, and even from some of their discussions and appointed readings. Thus the worshipper in the church pew on Sunday mornings is listening to carefully selected—and sometimes slightly edited—readings. Even the American *Book of Common Prayer* is not above this little bit of trickery.* And Episcopalians are supposed to be among America's more enlightened religionists.

The purpose of this book is to inform the reader as

*For example, the gory ending of Psalm 137 and the shocking verses from the story of Lot in Sodom, among other readings, are directed to be omitted at church services.

to the genuinely human interest that the Bible has in the whole subject of sex. Hopefully it will not turn anyone away from the Bible. On the contrary, if readers go through this book with any diligence they will refer to their Bibles again and again and check out not only each marginal reference but the whole context of the citation as well.

The Old Testament was originally written in Hebrew and the New Testament in Greek. Occasionally this must be mentioned, but no more often than essential, as this book was planned not for the specialist but for the general reader. You, the reader, are to accompany your perusal with any translation of the Bible that you like (but beware of variant verse numberings if you are using the *Douay Version*). My own preference for quoting the *Revised Standard Version* in the text is probably because I have become accustomed to it after using it in teaching for twenty years. Then again, it doesn't differ so much from the familiar *King James*.

The Bible is a treasure-house of knowledge. It represents life, which is beautiful, exquisite, and tender, and sometimes quite ordinary, ugly, and painful. It is life as it is—never *la vie en rose*.

There may be those who feel that I have failed to see human love in the context of the divine love. My answer to that is that divine love is not the subject of this book. However when the Old Testament wanted to speak of God's love for his people, it used the figure of "the husband" (Hos. 2). God was "the husband," Israel "the bride." Thus even divine love in the Bible was portrayed under an image of physical love.

In view of the current emphasis on women's rights, perhaps some readers will feel that this book should include a separate chapter on the Bible's attitude toward woman. Actually there is no one attitude, there are many. There is quite a lot of material on the subject, and much of it is mentioned in these pages. Every strand of information pertaining to women is not included for the simple reason that this is not the main subject of the book. Furthermore, to assess the attitudes toward this topic in works such as Proverbs and the apocryphal book of Ecclesiasticus alone would require a large essay or two, not to mention the epistles of Paul. In any case, the subject here is never discussed as an isolated topic but in conjunction with every one of the headings listed in the Contents, wherever it is relevant. The topic is neither avoided nor highlighted. Readers who may wish to pursue the subject further will find ample material here with which to begin their research.

Also, there is no separate chapter on the subject of love-making. Topics related to love-making are treated in various chapters throughout the book. Furthermore, the techniques of the ancients in this regard did not differ substantially from ours. Where differences do occur, attention has been called to them in the text. The best guide to the subject of love-making, however, is to be found in the Song of Solomon, which begins:

> O that you would kiss me with the kisses of
> your mouth!
> For your love is better than wine.
>
> —*Song of Solomon 1:2*

The Bible is, after all, a very sexy book.

TOM HORNER

Saratoga Springs, N. Y.

KEY TO MARGINAL REFERENCES

Gen..... Genesis
Exod. .. Exodus
Lev. .... Leviticus
Num. ... Numbers
Deut. ... Deuteronomy
Josh..... Joshua
Judg. ... Judges
Ruth .... Ruth
I Sam. .. I Samuel
II Sam. . II Samuel
I Kgs.... I Kings
II Kgs... II Kings
Esth.... Esther
Job .... Job
Ps. ..... Psalms
Prov. .. Proverbs
Eccl.... Ecclesiastes
Song.... Song of Solomon
Isa. ..... Isaiah
Jer. .... Jeremiah
Lam.... Lamentations
Ezek. ... Ezekiel
Hos. .... Hosea
Joel..... Joel
Amos. .. Amos
Mal..... Malachi
Matt. ..... Matthew
Mark ..... Mark
Luke ..... Luke
John...... John
Acts...... The Acts
Rom. ..... Romans
I Cor...... I Corinthians
II Cor..... II Corinthians
Gal. ...... Galatians
Eph. ...... Ephesians
Col. ...... Colossians
I Thes. .... I Thessalonians
I Tim. .... I Timothy
Tit........ Titus
Jas........ James
I Pet. ..... I Peter
I John.... I John
Rev. ...... The Revelation

FROM THE APOCRYPHA

Tob. ...... Tobit
Judith. .... Judith
Add. Esth. Additions to Esther
Ecclus..... Ecclesiasticus
Sus. ...... Susanna
I Macc. ... I Maccabees

1

MARRIAGE

HUMAN SEXUALITY is not only endorsed but commanded in the very first chapter of the
Gen. 1:27–28 Bible. "God created man in his own image. . . . male and female he created them." Then he said to them, "Be fruitful and multiply and fill the earth and subdue it. . . ." Both sexes were created on the same day.

In the second chapter of Genesis the story of creation is repeated, but this time it is related somewhat differently. The man was created first. Then, after reflecting that it was not a good thing for the man to be alone, God caused him to fall into a deep sleep and took one of his ribs and created woman. She was promptly presented to the man, who said:

Gen. 2:23

This at last is bone of my bones
  and flesh of my flesh;
she shall be called Woman,
  because she was taken out of Man.

Gen. 2:24–25 Therefore, we are told, "a man leaves his father and his mother and cleaves to his wife, and they become one flesh. And the man and his wife were both naked, and were not ashamed."

There is no evidence that the man or the woman had one rib more than the other, nor have they ever had. The story is really told to explain something else, namely sin. For no sooner was the woman created, as this story has it, than she proceeded to lead her husband into temptation and sin. It was she who partook of the forbidden fruit first and then gave it to her husband.* The fruit in question was not necessarily an apple. We are only told that it
Gen. was a fruit that was "good for food, a delight
3:6 to the eyes, and to be desired to make one
wise." And, also, that it was from the Tree of the Knowledge of Good and Evil. When they ate of it, the text says that "the eyes of both
Gen. were opened, and they knew that they were
3:7 naked; and they sewed fig leaves together and
made themselves aprons." Biblical critics have assumed that the knowledge that they received here was a sexual awareness. This would imply that heretofore they did not possess such knowledge. The experience could also represent the loss of innocence, the bloom of youth, or of any previous state of life to which one cannot return.

The woman's punishment for her part in this celebrated incident was, first of all, pain in childbirth ("in pain shall you bring forth

*Recently I was told that this proves that the desire for knowledge (with all that this implies) is stronger in women than in men. But it is doubtful that the Biblical writers had this in mind.

children") and, secondly, submission to male domination. She was told:

> *Gen.* Yet your desire shall be for your husband,
> *3:16* and he shall rule over you.

So it has been ever since in the Middle East, and some would say elsewhere.

But another thing that we should keep in mind as we read on in the Old Testament is the identification here of "knowledge" with "sex." Genesis, chapter four, begins: "Now Adam
Gen. *knew* Eve his wife and she conceived and bore
4:1 Cain." Note again the verb "to know" or one of its derivatives used as a euphemism for sexual intercourse. And note that it says that a child was born of this union. Is Genesis trying to tell us that the sexual act was to take place only for the procreation of children? Some have thought so; but it is not necessary to read this implication into the text. We do know that the Biblical writers were well aware that the sexual act produced children. And elsewhere in the Bible—especially in a little book called the Song of Solomon—it is made quite clear that sex is also for enjoyment.

Another interesting thing here is the use of
Gen. the specific designations "husband" and
2:24–25 "wife." Several times throughout this nar-
3:6 rative the world's first pair are referred to by
3:16 these terms. Eve, the "mother of all living,"
4:1 was especially created for Adam, the first man; hence it was a union with divine sanction. But

whenever in the Old Testament a man and a woman were paired off and given to each other to live together, it was a marriage.

There is a saying that marriages are made in
heaven and perhaps this is true, for marriages
in the Bible never needed clergymen to perform
them. The arrangements were made by the
Matt. respective families. At the wedding the bride-
25:6–10 groom was escorted rather ceremoniously to
his waiting bride, who was taken first to the
marriage feast and later to her husband's tent
Gen. or household where the marriage was con-
29:27 summated. The families and invited guests
Judg. stayed for further feasting that could last
14:12 anywhere from seven to fourteen days. Tradi-
Tob. tion has it that one of the women guests or
8:19 relatives checked on the couple occasionally to
see that things were progressing properly in
regard to the consummation of the marriage.
She then reported to the other guests, who
followed it all with great interest as they
continued with their feast.* The food was
provided usually by the family of the groom;
but special situations could sometimes dictate
otherwise. In any case he was expected to pay
Gen. something to the relatives of the girl in ex-
34:12 change for her. Daughters were considered to

*This is not documented in Holy Scripture except indirectly in the apocryphal book of Tobit, where there are extenuating circumstances. The book of Tobit is considered to be fully canonical by some Protestant churches, and is often found in their Bibles—it is always in Roman Catholic Bibles. In any event, the book is invaluable for the study of marriage in Biblical times.

I Sam. be a part of their father's property and were
18:25 not to be had for nothing.

We have mentioned that marriages were arranged by the parents in the ancient Middle East, as they still are in certain quarters there. Often the young man would have some say
Judg. in the matter; the girl almost never. When
14:2 Samson saw one of the daughters of the Philistines that pleased him, he said to his parents, "Now get her for me as my wife." Saul's daughter Michal was much taken with David when she
I Sam. first met him, but she could not have become
18:20 his wife without her father's permission.

Laban the Aramean made the complete arrangements for the marriage of his sister Rebekah to Abraham's son Isaac and then
Gen. turned to the girl and said, "Will you go with
24:58 this man?" She answered, "I will go," which was a good thing, for it does not appear that she would have had any choice in the matter anyway. Furthermore, "the man" to whom Laban referred in his question was really not the groom but Abraham's steward, who was making the arrangements from the groom's side. The girl had not yet seen her prospective husband, Isaac.

The account of Isaac's first meeting with his bride is totally charming and reveals at the same time how quickly the young people got down to the business of what marriage was all about. This is the way the Bible presents it:

> And Isaac went out to meditate in the field

> in the evening; and he lifted up his eyes and looked, and behold, there were camels coming. And Rebekah lifted up her eyes, and when she saw Isaac, she alighted from *Gen. 24:63–67* the camel, and said to the servant, "Who is the man yonder, walking in the field to meet us?" The servant said, "It is my master." So she took her veil and covered herself. And the servant told Isaac all the things that he had done. Then Isaac brought her into his tent, and took Rebekah, and she became his wife; and he loved her. So Isaac was comforted after his mother's death.

Note that love here comes after marriage, not before. This is the usual Eastern way. There are exceptions, such as Jacob's love for Rachel for seven years before he actually married her. *Gen. 29:20* We are told that "they seemed to him but a few days because of the love he had for her." But we are never really told that she loved him. In fact, we are never told that any man and woman in the Bible were "in love" with each other. The concept of "falling in love" did not exist. To love in the Bible (or in Biblical times) meant to be strongly attached to a person, place, or thing;* and it was an attachment that

*The definition treats of God as Person. Those who do not believe that "love" in the Bible has to do with places and things should see Psalms 26:8, Luke 11:43, and numerous other references. The love of things is usually spoken of disparagingly, but not always; see for example, Genesis 27:4. In II Samuel 13:4 the verb "to love" clearly means "to lust after." Examples are numerous.

was far more physical than abstract. Sometimes
the more delicate emotional aspects of love
were present in a marriage, sometimes not.
But the physical attachment was always there,
even when the marriage was completely arranged, which was usually the case.

In the apocryphal book of Tobit there is a
Tob. reference to a written marriage contract. There
7:14 is also a reference to the young couple's
spending their first night in bed. But before
8:4 they retired for the evening the groom said,
"Sister, get up, and let us pray that the Lord
may have mercy upon us." He offered a prayer.
She said, "Amen." And then they went off to
sleep.

There were several peculiar Israelite customs
Deut. in regard to marriage. One was that a newly-
24:5 married man was exempt from military service
for one year, in order that he could "be happy
with the wife he has taken." Another reference
supporting this legislation—and it was a law—
Deut. said that this *must* be done in the case of a
20:7 betrothed man "lest he die in battle and another
man take her."

Another custom was that a woman captured
as a prize of war might be taken as a wife, but
not until she had been allowed to remain
untouched in the man's home for one full
month in order to "bewail her father and her
mother." Then he could take her. But, if after
Deut. the first month of marriage the husband was
21:10–14 dissatisfied with his captive bride, he must "let
her go where she will." He could not now sell

her as a slave (which apparently he could have done before taking her as a wife).

The most unusual of all the Israelite marriage customs from our point of view was something known as the Law of Levirate Marriage. The technical name that scholars use to describe this law is taken from the Latin word *levir*, meaning "the husband's brother." This custom is older than the Law of Moses, for it is mentioned in the Bible beginning in the days of the patriarchs in the book of Genesis. It is best explained where it is enunciated in the Deuteronomic code as follows:

> If brothers dwell together, and one of them dies and has no son, the wife of the dead shall not be married outside the family to a stranger; her husband's brother shall go in to her, and take her as his wife, and perform the duty of a husband's brother to her. And the first son whom she bears shall succeed to the name of his brother who is dead, that his name may not be blotted out of Israel. And if the man does not wish to take his brother's wife, then his brother's wife shall go up to the gate to the elders, and say, "My husband's brother refuses to perpetuate his brother's name in Israel; he will not perform the duty of a husband's brother to me." Then the elders of his city shall call him, and speak to him: and if he persists, saying, "I do not wish to take her," then his brother's wife shall go up to him in the presence

Deut. 25:5–10

> of the elders, and pull his sandal off his foot, and spit in his face; and she shall answer and say, "So shall it be done to the man who does not build up his brother's house." And the name of his house shall be called in Israel, The house of him that had his sandal pulled off.

This strange custom actually had two very useful functions. First of all, it provided a child for the poor childless widow, who in the normal course of events would not be acceptable as the wife of another. Men who had anything to do with the selection of a wife for themselves in the Middle East invariably picked virgins, or thought they did. Therefore the widow's chances were rather slim. Secondly, the system of levirate marriage provided for the deceased brother the most important memorial in the world from society's point of view—that was a child, if only by proxy. However, it should be made quite clear that the Bible indicates that the brother's widow need not have been the only wife for the second brother. She remained simply as an additional member of his or of his father's household. Thus the whole idea would have been quite unthinkable without the assumption beforehand of the extended family concept.

One of the best examples of levirate marriage is in the story of Judah and Tamar in Genesis, chapter thirty-eight, which we will discuss in another connection. It occurs also throughout

the little book of Ruth, and the story there is incomprehensible unless one understands the concept of levirate marriage. Even in the New Testament we come across it in one of
Matt. 22:23–30 the enigmatic questions put to Jesus by the Sadducees in order to get him into a legal bind. As usual he evaded them with a cryptic answer.

The book of Proverbs abounds in references to women and marriage, so many in fact that it would take us completely away from our subject to mention them all. But most relevant to our discussion here, the author admonishes his readers (male, of course):

Prov. 5:18–19

> Let your fountain be blessed,
> and rejoice in the wife of your youth,
> a lovely hind, a graceful doe.
> Let her affection fill you at all times
> with delight,
> be infatuated always with her love.

Prov. 31:10–31 The book ends with a long poem in praise of the virtuous wife, who merits the praise because she relieves her husband of all tedious work.

Eccl. 9:9 Ecclesiastes admonishes its male readers: "Enjoy life with the wife whom you love." And the little book called Song of Solomon, more than any other in the whole Bible, places its emphasis entirely along the same lines. We shall have more to say about this unique work in further chapters.

When we come to the New Testament there

is much less talk of "enjoying" the wife whom you have married. Because many of the New Testament writers believed that they were living near the end of time, tolerating what one must in the interim was more down their line. This attitude was more openly expressed after the life of Jesus, during the advent of the early church. His emphasis was primarily upon the indissolubility of marriage, about which we will have more to say later. The Apostle Paul, however, who showed a much greater concern for sexual topics anyway, had a lot to say.

First of all, the unmarried and widows he advises to remain as they are. But, he says, if they cannot exercise self-control, then they
I Cor. should marry: "For it is better to marry than
7:9 to be aflame with passion." The *King James Version* has here: "It is better to marry than to burn." Even before getting around to this sage advice Paul had warned that "because of
I Cor. the temptation to immorality, each man should
7:2 have his own wife and each woman her own husband." He continues:

> The husband should give to his wife her conjugal rights, and likewise the wife to her husband. For the wife does not rule over her
> *I Cor.* own body, but the husband does; likewise
> *7:3–5* the husband does not rule over his own body, but the wife does. Do not refuse one another except by agreement for a season . . . "

Notice the words above that state that they

should give to each other their "conjugal
rights." This passage has influenced many
civil marriage laws, which go so far as to state
that if he or she does not "give it," then the
other party may use this as grounds for divorce.

But we find some ambiguity in Paul, too, for
further down in the same chapter he advises
I Cor. that in view of the impending end of the world
7:26 those who have spouses should live as if they
had none. In other words, he was suggesting
complete continence. Here, as elsewhere, Paul
revealed himself to be rather prudish in his
sexual attitudes. For example, he told the men
of the Thessalonian church to abstain from
I Thes. promiscuity and "to take a wife for himself
4:4–5 in holiness and honor, not in the passion of
lust like heathen who do not know God . . . "

We also find another kind of ambiguity in
Gal. Paul, and that is in his attitude toward women.
3:28 On the one hand he wrote that in Christ Jesus
"there is neither male nor female," which seems
to imply some kind of equality. Was he saying
that real Christianity should eradicate the
barriers that separate people? If so, then he
meant only certain barriers. For on the other
I Cor. hand he said that women should keep their
14:34–35 mouths shut in church. "If there is anything
they desire to know, let them ask their husbands at home." Of course he was speaking in
this context only in regard to matters of church;
but one gets the feeling that the same attitude
would spill over into other areas as well. For
elsewhere he told them that a man "is the

I Cor. image and glory of God; but woman is the glory
11:7–9 of man. . . . (Neither was man created for woman, but woman for man.)" The same advice about women keeping silent in church is found again in First Timothy, the first of the so-called Pastoral Epistles—which may or may not be by Paul, depending upon
I Tim. whichever one of the scholarly opinions one
2:12–15 chooses to hold on the subject. First Timothy adds, furthermore: "I permit no woman to teach or to have authority over men . . . Yet woman will be saved through bearing children, if she continues in faith and love and holiness, with modesty."

The Epistle to the Ephesians, according to scholarly opinion, also may or may not be by Paul. Probably not, for it is much harder on women than the works that we know to be by Paul.* It says:

> Wives, be subject to your husbands, as to the Lord. For the husband is the head of the wife as Christ is the head of the church, his body, and is himself its Savior. As the church is
> *Eph.* subject to Christ, so let wives also be subject
> *5:22–28* in everything to their husbands. Husbands, love your wives, as Christ loved the church and gave himself up for her. . . . Even so husbands should love their wives as their own bodies. He who loves his wife loves himself.

*Romans, I–II Corinthians, Galatians, Philippians, Colossians, I–II Thessalonians, and Philemon.

The difference is that here wives are to "be subject to" their husbands.

The little Epistle to Titus says that wives
Tit. 2:5 should be "submissive to their husbands,"
and four verses further down in the same
2:9 chapter, that slaves should be "submissive to
their masters." The First Epistle of Peter
I Pet. 3:1 bids that wives should be submissive to their
husbands, and also that husbands should act
with consideration toward their wives, "be-
3:7 stowing honor on the woman as the weaker
sex." This goes all the way back to the idea of male domination expressed at the beginning of the book of Genesis. It is the Old Testament idea of the patriarchal society still present in the Bible to the end.

What if a person chose not to marry? This was almost unheard of. As we have said before, a man or woman did not have to go out and look for a wife or husband. This was done for them by their families. Of course a homely girl was the last to be chosen. Often a pretty girl was used as a pawn. Her father, seeking some favor, might give her to a king or chieftain as a gift. There was nothing the girl could do about it. It was a union of families and nothing was more important than these alliances. Even priests and prophets were married. Of the four Old Testament prophets about whom we have the most biographical
Jer. 16:2 information—Hosea, Isaiah, Jeremiah, and
Ezekiel—only Jeremiah chose not to marry.
And he, in the course of one of his public

oracles, felt called upon to explain that the reason for his self-imposed bachelorhood was
Matt. the impending doom. Simon Peter, supposedly
8:14 the first pope, was married or had been mar-
I Cor. ried, for he had a mother-in-law! The Apostle
7:8 Paul appears to have been single when he made his great missionary journeys, but we do not know that he always had been. There is a lot about Paul that we do not know.*

What we do know is that marriage was the Biblical ideal, with the man as the head of a family, a family that sometimes included more than one wife.

*For instance, what was his "thorn in the flesh," which he refers to so mysteriously in II Corinthians 12;7?

2

POLYGAMY

THE OLD TESTAMENT from the outset presents
polygamy without editorial comment. We are
not told that it is right or wrong, good or bad.
We simply learn who had more than one wife.
In one of the earliest chapters of Genesis we
Gen. are informed that Lamech, a close descendant
4:19 of Cain, had two wives, Adah and Zillah, to
both of whom the boastful Lamech sang a
proud and bloodthirsty song.

In regard to the partriarch Abraham, the
text specifically impresses upon us that the
Gen. lovely Sarah was his *principal* wife, and it is
11:31 from her that the Israelites are descended. But
the book of Genesis plainly says that he took
Gen. another wife, Keturah, who bore him several
25:1–6 children. Not only this, but because of his first
wife's childlessness, and with her permission,
he enjoyed the affections of her maidservant,
Gen. Hagar, by whom he also had a child. This
16:12 "wild ass of a man"—and that is just the way
he is described—became the ancestor of all the
Arabs. The Old Testament, in grand style,

makes no editorial comment about polygamy
in connection with any of this.

The good Isaac, son of Abraham and Sarah,
Gen. had only one wife, Rebekah, and the story of
24 their betrothal and marriage is one of the most
delightful chapters in the Bible The whole
thing was arranged by others, and yet it seemed
to work out well enough. The two sons of this
marriage, however, were quite polygamous.

Esau, the elder, had three wives who bore
Gen. him many children, and one whole chapter of
36 the book of Genesis is taken up with the list of
his descendants. His brother Jacob started out
in pursuit of only one wife, Rachel, but he ended
up with four. The last two, being slaves of the
first two, are sometimes thought of and referred
Gen. to as concubines instead of as wives. Con-
30:4 cubinage has been defined as: "cohabitation of
30:9 persons not legally married."* However this may
31:17 be, the text of Genesis refers to them as "wives."

It happened in this way. Jacob loved Rachel
upon first sight and contracted to work seven
years for her. Because the brides were veiled,
the father-in-law was able to trick Jacob into
going through with a wedding ceremony that
married him to the older sister, Leah, although
the unsuspecting groom was not to learn this
Gen. until the next day. The text says: "In the
29:25 morning, behold, it was Leah." Jacob complained but to no avail. The father said, "It is
not so done in our country to give the younger

* *Webster's Seventh New Collegiate Dictionary*, 1971 (hereafter cited as *Webster's*, 1971).

before the first-born." So, Jacob contracted to work another seven years for Rachel. Contrary to the way most people interpret this text, he did not have to wait another seven years before having her. He simply had to wait out the week, which was the wedding feast to which Leah was entitled, mistake or not. He did, however, have to work out the additional seven years' labor.

Leah had several children, but the beloved Rachel was at first childless. Therefore she
Gen. offered her husband her maid "to wife," so that
30:3–4 "even I may have children through her." Jacob accepted and two sons were born of this union. Not to be outdone by her sister in this respect, Leah also gave Jacob her maid with the same idea in mind. The question is never raised that the same reasoning would not be valid, for Leah already had children in her own right. Jacob was nevertheless obliging, and more children were born. Finally Rachel had children after all, which, if she had done so in the first
30:22 place, would have made all of this unnecessary. But perhaps the story is told simply to explain how Jacob ended up with four wives.

Moses himself had two wives, which may
Exod. clarify why there is no legislation in his law
2:21 about husbands having only one. His first wife
Num. was a typical bedouin (but non-Israelite) girl,
12:1 while his second wife was black (a Cushite).

His law does say, however, that if a man
Exod. "takes another wife to himself, he shall not
21:10 diminish her food, her clothing, or her marital rights." This law was written in the context of

a man's taking a concubine or female slave as an "extra wife," but surely the requirement about giving to each one her "marital rights" would apply to any other wife as well. Such an obligation, as well as the economic reasons usually cited, would have prevented the average man, if he were at all considerate, from marrying too often.

Elkanah, the father of the prophet Samuel, had two wives, but one of them, Peninnah, was quite a bitch! Although blessed with children herself, she constantly chided and irritated her husband's other wife, Hannah, who was barren. "So it went on year by year," until God himself finally intervened in the matter. We can easily see from this account how polygamy could make for a miserable situation within the family. But things could be even worse. In the case of the next person we shall consider, his sons by one wife murdered his sons by another. This was David.

I Sam. 1:2–20

King David had eight wives. Their names were Michal, Ahinoam, Abigail, Maacah, Haggith, Abital, Eglah, and Bathsheba. The last of these has been the most celebrated in fiction and in film, both mostly fiction. But it is not fiction that David's son by Maacah murdered his son by Ahinoam, and his son by Bathsheba murdered his son by Haggith. Somewhere in this we should see an argument against polygamy.

II Sam. 3:2–5

David is also said to have had concubines. Some of these, and some of his wives as well, could have been gifts from neighboring kings and chieftains, as the giving of females as gifts was the custom among kings. And even if a king had not wanted the particular addition to his harem, protocol would have demanded that he accept the gift anyway.

David's illustrious son Solomon topped everyone in the number of wives he accumulated, as in everything else. It is said that he had seven hundred of them, plus three hundred concubines. This has given rise to the popular belief that King Solomon had a thousand wives. The many foreign wives, according to the text, alienated Solomon from his God, and the kingdom split into two parts after his death.

I Kgs. 11:3

Long before we come to the time of the New Testament the Jews seemed to have settled down to the idea that one wife at a time was sufficient for their needs. And Christianity, as in most other things pertaining to Jewish morality, of course followed suit. But the practice of monogamy was apparently arrived at by the process of expediency rather than by legislation. Custom, as is usually true, was more powerful than law; and in this case the custom eventually became the law. Anyway, both Judaism and Christianity were then living in the midst of a Greek and Roman world that was also monogamous.

Of course Jesus Christ's stance on monogamy comes out quite clearly within the context of his attitude toward divorce. This topic must now be considered.

3

DIVORCE

THE OLD TESTAMENT not only acknowledges divorce; it even makes provision for a written contract to that effect. But only a husband could seek it; a wife could not institute the proceedings. Called a "bill of divorce" in the
Deut. 24:1–4 Deuteronomic legislation and elsewhere, it does contain some special stipulations. A divorced woman could marry another or she could remarry her former husband. But if she had married another man, she could never go back to her former husband even though the second one might have died in the meantime.

The cause for which a man might seek a divorce, as stated in Deuteronomy, was rather flimsy. It simply says that he has cause if "she finds no favor in his eyes because he has found some indecency in her." It implies, however, that this complaint should be forthcoming in the early stages of the marriage. Unless she were guilty of some gross infidelity, it is difficult to imagine the average man of the Bible, of the Old Testament period especially, sending away the mother of his children. Family solidarity ran high and loyalties, as a rule, were strong. On the other hand, a woman who wanted a divorce badly enough might have been able to provoke her husband into seeking one.

We have no way of knowing the frequency
of divorce in the Bible, as the only references to
it are of a general nature. But there must have
been some occurrences, or there would have
been no occasion for the general references at
Lev. all. For instance, the text says that a priest's
22:13 daughter who is divorced may return to her
father's house for board; that the divorced
Num. woman must stand good for a vow made,
30:9 even if it was made while she was married to
her former husband. Finally, it says that no
Lev. priest is to marry a divorced woman. Neither
21:14 can he marry a widow or a harlot! All of this
points out that there must have been some
Judg. divorced women around.

15:2 There were two men—Samson and David—
II Sam. who had their first wives taken away from them
3:13–16 by their fathers-in-law. But both these cases
were peculiar because of extenuating circumstances and need not be taken as representative.

What we must take much more seriously is
that the prophet Malachi toward the end of the
Old Testament inveighs against divorce in
Mal. general. At first he seems to be against divorce
2:11 that occurs so that a man can marry a non-
Israelitish wife, "the daughter of a foreign
god." But later he quotes God as saying, "I
2:15–16 hate divorce," and "let none be faithless to the
wife of his youth." In spite of the clarity of the

prophet's language here, some scholars say that he was speaking only of religious apostasy.

When we come to the New Testament there is quite a strong statement from Jesus on the subject:

> It was also said, "Whoever divorces his wife,
> let him give her a certificate of divorce." But
> I say to you that every one who divorces his
> *Matt.* wife, except on the ground of unchastity,
> *5:31–32* makes her an adulteress; and whoever mar-
> ries a divorced woman commits adultery.

Mark Mark has Jesus say here that "if she divorces
10:12 her husband and marries another, she commits adultery." We are curious as to why he would say that. Women could not sue for divorce in Palestine. Was he thinking of the wider context of the Graeco-Roman world where this was possible? Or did he forget for a moment that women did not possess equal rights with men?

We can be very sure the Pharisees did not forget it, as witnessed by the way they phrased the following question to him: "Is it lawful to divorce one's wife for any cause?" He answered:

> Have you not read that he who made them
> from the beginning made them male and
> *Matt.* female, and said, "For this reason a man shall
> *19:4–5* leave his father and mother and be joined
> to his wife, and the two shall become one"?
> So they are no longer two but one. What

> therefore God has joined together, let no man put asunder.

Jesus' stand against divorce at once recognized the solidarity of the family and protected the woman from abandonment. There is a kind of recognition of an equality of the sexes in his answer. Each partner is equally an object of concern. When asked why Moses had allowed divorce in the first place, he answered that it
Matt. was because of "your hardness of heart" at the
19:8 time.

The Apostle Paul too is against divorce. But,
I Cor. he says, if Christians must do it, they are not
7:11 to remarry—unless they decide to get married again to each other.

One of the latest books to be written in the New Testament contains the curious remark
I Tim. that bishops and deacons should be "married
3:2 only once," which means not only that they
3:12 might not divorce one wife for another but that if the first wife died there was to be no second.

4

CONSANGUINITY AND INCEST

CONSANGUINITY is defined as "the quality or state of being consanguineous," which in turn means "of the same blood or origin"; specifically, "descended from the same ancestor." The Bible sets up restrictions on consanguineous sex. These restrictions, however, were not always observed. Even *incest,* or "sexual relations between persons so closely related that they are forbidden by law to marry," appears far more often than we would imagine—until the record is examined.*

The restrictions, as worded in the Old Testament, very quaintly say that "you shall not uncover the nakedness of" such and such persons. But this is simply the Biblical way of saying that you shall not marry them or have sexual intercourse with them at any time. The section begins: "None of you shall approach any one near of kin *to him,*" and then goes on to single out twelve prohibitions. A man is told that he is not to cohabit with:

*Definitions in this paragraph are from *Webster's*, 1971.

1. his mother;
2. his father's wife (in cases in which she is not his own mother);
3. his sister;
4. his son's daughter or his daughter's daughter;
5. his father's wife's daughter (in cases in which she is his half-sister);

Lev. 18:6–18

6. his father's sister;
7. his mother's sister;
8. the wife of his father's brother;
9. his daughter-in-law;
10. his brother's wife (the custom of levirate marriage, or the duty of a brother to "raise up offspring" for his deceased brother, was obviously an exception here);
11. any woman *and* her daughter or granddaughter;
12. any woman as a rival wife to her sister "while her sister is yet alive."

Although addressed to men, the laws would apply equally to women in most cases, for a woman could not cohabit with a man if the degree of her relationship to him would fall under any of the above categories. But there are some inequities. Although a boy is told that he cannot cohabit with his aunt, a girl is not told that she cannot have intercourse with her uncle, and, for that matter, with her own father. Could it be that the introductory verse, which referred to "any one near of kin," was meant to cover these omissions? Not necessarily, for the Old Testament codes containing ten or twelve laws are frequently preceded by a sentence introduction that is simply meant to be descriptive or to serve as a kind of preamble of the enumerated laws that follow.

Exod. 20:2 For example, the Ten Commandments are introduced by such a preamble. Furthermore, in these cases, the ten or twelve laws are usually cast in the same literary form whereas the preamble will utilize a variant form. Both of these factors are present here. Thus the introduction (verse six) is most likely *not* one of the code's laws. Then why the omissions? Was it because the possibility of violating virgins was circumvented by other legislation? Or did they think that cases of a man taking his own daughter or niece would not arise? Certainly the great value placed upon virginity in the young girls of one's own family would have made such a thing unthinkable to almost any man of their society.

Regardless of our faultfinding with the laws here, later societies have interpreted them to mean that no one—man or woman—was to marry or have intercourse with anyone who was closely related to him or her by blood or by marriage, and the marriage laws of numerous churches and states largely reflect this thinking. Strangely enough, the code says nothing about cousins, and the Bible is full of cousinly marriages.

Whereas it states quite clearly that sexual relations between such and such persons were prohibited, the code here says nothing of what the punishment would have been if the laws were broken. But as we read on a few chapters in the text, we find some statements more specific in this regard. Death was decreed for both parties in cases in which a man took the following:

Lev. 20:11–14

1. his father's wife (in any case);
2. his daughter-in-law;
3. a wife *and her mother also* (presumably at or near the same time).

Deut. 27:23

Under other conditions one who "lies with his mother-in-law" was not to be killed but was only accursed. This too, however, was a terrible thing in their world. It meant that he (and possibly she) would be anathema to the whole community, or, in other words, a social outcast.

Lev. 20:17

Finally, one who "takes his sister, a daughter of his father, or a daughter of his mother, and sees her nakedness" was to be excommunicated.

So much for the laws designed to prevent consanguineous sex and incest. Now for examples of what actually happened.

Going back to the early chapters of Genesis (which of course were before the laws were in effect), the Bible never really says where Cain got his wife. This is a question that vexes

teachers of the Bible no end, because they are invariably asked and can never answer the question. Presumably there was another child of Adam and Eve, an unnamed sister of Cain
Gen. who became his wife, or else there were other
4:17 people around.

Of course after the Great Flood the whole
Gen. human family, according to the Bible, started
9:18–19 all over again with three couples, the three
sons of Noah and their wives.

According to the genealogical tables of Genesis, Abraham represented the tenth generation after Noah, through Noah's son Shem. Thus Abraham was to be the progenitor of a large number of Semites, including both Arabs and Jews. Abraham married Sarai or Sarah, his half-sister. Although we are not told this in chapter eleven, where Abraham is introduced, it is revealed later, when he says to a petty king who was about to take away his wife:

> Besides she is indeed my sister, the daughter
> *Gen.* of my father but not the daughter of my
> *20:12* mother; and she became my wife.

Rebekah, the wife who was selected for Isaac,
Gen. was really his first cousin once removed, as
24:15 Bethuel her father was the first cousin of
Abraham, Isaac's father. But this did not stand in the way of the marriage. In fact, from their point of view it was an advantage. At least they knew who they were getting. Bedouins or

Gen. 29:1–30

Semitic-speaking nomads—and this is what the Hebrews before Joshua were—often married their cousins. Even the later laws did not forbid it. Jacob married not one but two of his cousins, Leah and Rachel. His mother and their father were sister and brother. And, contrary to the later law, he married the second one "while her sister was yet alive." Their progeny was eight of the twelve tribes of Israel.

Some of the other close relationships described in the Bible were not so acceptable by any standards. Nevertheless they happened. One of the lurid stories has to do with the origins of the nations of Moab and Ammon. They were descended from Lot, Abraham's nephew, but the circumstances of the descent were unusual. It happened in this way:

Gen. 19:30–38

> Now Lot went up out of Zoar, and dwelt in the hills with his two daughters, for he was afraid to dwell in Zoar; so he dwelt in a cave with his two daughters. And the first-born said to the younger, "Our father is old, and there is not a man on earth to come in to us after the manner of all the earth. Come, let us make our father drink wine, and we will lie with him, that we may preserve offspring through our father." So they made their father drink wine that night; and the first-born went in, and lay with her father; he did not know when she lay down or when she arose. And on the next day, the first-born said to the younger, "Behold, I lay last night

> with my father; let us make him drink wine tonight also; then you go in and lie with him, that we may preserve offspring through our father." So they made their father drink wine that night also; and the younger arose, and lay with him; and he did not know when she lay down or when she arose. Thus both the daughters of Lot were with child by their father. The first-born bore a son, and called his name Moab; he is the father of the Moabites to this day. The younger also bore a son, and called his name Ben-Ammi; he is the father of the Ammonites to this day.

Reuben, Jacob's oldest son, knowingly slept
Gen. with one of his father's wives, Bilhah, although
35:22 this time the Bible refers to her as a concubine.

The patriarch Judah had intercourse with
his own daughter-in-law, Tamar. But to his
Gen. credit it should be pointed out that he did not
38:16 know that it was his daughter-in-law; she was
disguised as a harlot, and that is what he
thought he was getting. Later he found out
otherwise.

King David's oldest son Amnon feigned
illness and asked that his half-sister Tamar
II Sam. come and wait on him. No sooner had she
13:1–15 arrived than he forced her to have sexual relations with him. But this we shall discuss
further on in connection with seduction and
rape.

David's son Absalom "went in to his father's concubines" publicly more or less—in a tent

on the roof of his father's house "in the sight
II Sam. of all Israel." This was a symbolic act to indi-
16:22 cate that he had now taken over everything
that was his father's. Since this was what was
expected of him if he was really to prove that
he had assumed control of his father's kingdom, perhaps it was not considered to be a
breach of the laws against consanguinity. The
law seems to have caused problems only in the
cases of legal wives, not with concubines.

In the New Testament we have the story of
Herodias, the wife of Philip the tetrarch, who
divorced her husband and married his brother.
Mark For this act the stern John the Baptist railed
6:17–18 against her as well as against her new husband,
Herod. As far as the Levitical law was concerned, John was right; but because he would
not shut up about it, eventually it cost him his
6:22–28 head. The actual beheading took place immediately following Salome's famous dance, in
connection with which King Herod had made a
vow that he could not retract. The reviled
Herodias thus had her revenge. And, so far as
we know, she did not give up her "illegal"
husband.

Even in the early Christian church the Levitical law against uncovering the nakedness of a father's wife caused grave concern. For the Apostle Paul made quite an issue of it when a member of the church at Corinth and the man's youthful stepmother were living as husband and wife. Even the Roman laws at the time would have forbade their marriage.

But what bothered Paul most of all was that some of the members of the congregation were actually tolerant of the situation. He wrote to the church:

> It is actually reported that there is immorality among you, and of a kind that is not found even among pagans; for a man is living with his father's wife. And are you arrogant! Ought you not rather to mourn! Let him who has done this be removed from among you.
>
> For though absent in body I am present in spirit, and as if present, I have already pronounced judgment in the name of the Lord Jesus on the man who has done such a thing. When you are assembled, and my spirit is present, with the power of our Lord Jesus, you are to deliver this man to Satan for the destruction of the flesh, that his spirit may be saved in the day of the Lord Jesus.

I Cor. 5:1–8

All of this condemnation in the name of the Lord Jesus is rather interesting when one considers that, other than the money-changers in the temple, Jesus himself never condemned anyone except people who manifested the kind of strait-laced character that Paul exhibited here.

5

WIFE-STEALING*

When Abraham was sojourning in Egypt, so the narrative relates, no less a personage than the Pharaoh saw how beautiful Sarah was and took her for his wife. But the Lord afflicted the Egyptians with great plagues because of it; therefore the Pharaoh sent her back. We are not told whether or not he had relations with her. But because he says, "I took her for my wife," presumably he did. What is even more amazing about this account is that the Pharaoh, who was supposed to be the living incarnation of the divine Sun, would even have a conversation with an Asiatic shepherd, much less have relations with his wife.

Gen. 12:10–20

A few chapters later in Genesis we have another account. It is almost a repeat of the first one, except that this one is much more wordy. Again it was Abraham whose wife was

*For some of the ideas presented here and elsewhere in regard to the cultural relationships between ancient Israel and Greece, I am indebted to Cyrus H. Gordon, "Homer and the Bible: The Origin and Character of East Mediterranean Literature," in *Hebrew Union College Annual* 26 (1955), pp. 43–108.

abducted. But this time the villain was Abimelech, king of Gerar—wherever that is. Everything happened as before, except that, instead of the plagues, God appeared to Abimelech in a dream and told him what was
Gen. what. Again the wife was returned, but this
20:1–18 time it is carefully pointed out that Sarah had
not been touched in any way by the abductor.

An amazing thing in the preceding story is something that Abimelech said to Abraham
Gen. when they discussed why Abraham had not
20:9 told him that Sarah was his wife. He remarked,
"You have done to me things that ought not to be done." Strangely enough, that is the earliest expression in the history of the Bible of a community social ethic, and perhaps it is still the best expression of our own social ethic. The community dictates what is right or wrong at the moment. Try doing otherwise and see what happens.

The third time this story motif appears in the text it is just that—that is, the motif of the story only, without the usual abduction of the bride. This time it is Isaac who is about to have his wife stolen. While he was living for a time in the country of the Philistines, Isaac told people that his wife Rebekah was his sister,
Gen. "lest the men of the place should kill me . . .
26:6–11 for she was fair to look upon." After some time
the king, who was also named Abimelech, looked out his window and saw Isaac "fondling Rebekah his wife," and then the truth emerged. The king and Isaac exchanged words about it,

and that was the end of the episode. But in this case, as we have pointed out already, the bride was not actually abducted.

Again there is an amazing detail in addition to the usual near attempt to steal the wife. This time it is the presence of the people called Philistines. Although this was their later home—and they gave their name Philistia (Palestina) to the whole country—they could not possibly have been there as early as the time of Isaac, son of Abraham. These people of Aegean origin settled on the coast of Palestine during the Mediterranean upheavals that took place about the time of the Trojan War. But we can be sure that when they did come, they brought with them their own version of the famous story of the abducted bride. The motif of the stolen wife lies behind the whole story of the Trojan War and the *Iliad.* There is even a Canaanite version called the "Legend of King Keret." But in every one of them the ending is the same: the wife is invariably returned to her former husband.

The final instance of the wife-stealing theme in the Bible is in some material that scholars consider completely historical. It has to do with David's accession to the throne of Israel. David's first wife, Michal, the daughter of Saul, had been taken away from him after his defection from Israel's first king, and she had
II Sam. 3:13–16 been duly given to another. One of the conditions of David's kingship over united Israel was that she must be returned. The request was

granted by Abner, the Israeli commander-in-chief, although the woman's second husband, Paltiel, followed her "weeping . . . all the way to Bahurim." Then Abner said to him, "Go, return," and he returned. Here, as in the *Iliad*, the woman had been enjoyed as a wife during the interim.

6

ADULTERY AND FORNICATION

THERE IS one commandment that has caused more anxieties than any other for persons who take their commandments seriously and who
Exod. 20:14 are at the same time possessors of weak wills and lustful eyes. This is the seventh: "Thou
Deut. 5:18 shalt not commit adultery." *Adultery* is defined as "voluntary sexual intercourse between a married man and someone other than his wife or between a married woman and someone other than her husband." Adultery is often confused with *fornication*, which is "human sexual intercourse other than between a man and his wife."* Thus, single persons who have intercourse with partners, married or single, are only committing fornication.

But in the Old Testament all of this was not exactly interpreted as in *Webster's Seventh.* Wives were considered to be guilty of adultery if they had intercourse with any man other than their husbands; husbands, only if they had relations with another married woman. If

*Both definitions are from *Webster's*, 1971.

married men had extra-marital relations only with unmarried women, they were simply fornicating.

Strangely enough the Ten Commandments appear superficially to contain nothing about fornication. But the tenth and last commandment goes on to say that you (if you are a man) should not so much as "covet," or look with eyes of envy or desire in the direction
Exod. of "your neighbor's wife, or his manservant,
20:17 or his maidservant, or his ox, or his ass,
Deut. or anything that is your neighbor's." The
5:21 whole thing is obviously men writing to
men. And it certainly has some reference to fornication. For in a way a man is being told that he must not have anything such as fornication in mind when he looks over and beholds his neighbor's maidservant—and so on. But before anyone jumps to accuse Moses of an unbalanced concern with the subject of sex, it must be admitted that the main thrust of the tenth commandment is directed against envy and greed as concerns a neighbor's property. But, note again, that his wife is just as much a part of his property as his manservant or his ass. And although this commandment alone among the Ten appears to be addressed to men only, it perhaps has the protection of the women in mind.

Whereas adultery is simply forbidden by the
Lev. Ten Commandmants, in a couple of places
20:10 hidden away in the Levitical and Deuteronomic
codes the act was punishable by death for

both the adulterer and the adulteress, In that
Deut. 22:22 way, we are told, "you shall purge the evil from Israel."

There was even a test that a jealous husband could force his wife to undergo in cases of suspected adultery. Supposedly this would indicate her innocence or guilt in the matter. It becomes quite involved, covering almost one whole chapter. We shall quote only a part of it in order to give the reader some idea of the procedure the unfortunate woman might have to bear.

> Then the priest shall . . . make the woman drink the water of bitterness that brings the curse, and the water that brings the curse shall enter into her and cause bitter pain. And the priest shall take the cereal offering of jealousy out of the woman's hand, and shall wave the cereal offering before the LORD and bring it to the altar; and the
> *Num. 5:23–28* priest shall take a handful of the cereal offering, as its memorial portion, and burn it upon the altar, and afterward shall make the woman drink the water. And when he has made her drink the water, then, if she has defiled herself and has acted unfaithfully against her husband, the water that brings the curse shall enter into her and cause bitter pain, and her body shall swell, and her thigh shall fall away, and the woman shall become an execration among her people. But if the woman has not defiled herself and

is clean, then she shall be free and shall conceive children.

What the "water of bitterness" was, we do not know. But it must have been something quite potent to have had such devastating effects. There was no such test—indeed no test of any kind—for a man who was suspected of adultery.

There is a reason—and, from a man's point of view, a justifiable one—why adultery on the part of the female was (and is) taken more seriously than in the male: a woman always knows who her children are; but, in cases of his wife's infidelity, a man does not. This is perhaps relevant to the entire discussion but especially to the incident we are about to relate.

The most famous case of adultery in the Bible was that between David and Bathsheba. It all began late one afternoon when the king was walking on his roof and saw at some distance a woman bathing, "and the woman was very beautiful." He inquired who she was, and upon learning that her husband was one of his troops away in battle, he sent for her and "lay with her." When she became pregnant
II Sam. she notified David. He knew that the child
11:1–27 was his, but decided to try to pass it off on the husband if he could. The patriotic soldier was given a sudden leave of absence from the front, which he accepted; but he would not go in to visit his wife, choosing instead to sleep in the king's barracks for the duration of the furlough. There now seemed nothing left for

David to do but to order his commander to put Bathsheba's husband in the forefront of the fighting "so that he might be struck down and die." And so it was done. Then David took the lovely widow to wife. But, we are told, the thing that David had done displeased the LORD greatly. From that moment on, David's career was plagued with nothing but bad luck. This is the Old Testament's way of saying that you may sin against others if you choose to do so, but God will extract punishment in his own way. Of course the "sin" in this case was not only adultery but murder as well.

Some say that David wrote Psalm 51 with this particular incident in mind. Whoever
Ps. wrote it says, "In sin did my mother conceive
51:5 me," but the psalmist here may be thinking only of the universal human condition of sinfulness and not necessarily of his own mother's adultery.

When we come to the New Testament,
Matt. Jesus Christ said, "You have heard that it was
5:27–28 said, 'You shall not commit adultery.' But I say to you that every one who looks at a woman lustfully has already committed adultery with
Matt. her in his heart." In another speech he equated
15:19 adultery with "evil thoughts" that proceed from the heart and defile a person, whereas deeds that do not proceed from the heart do not defile.

One of the best known stories in the gospels—though it is highly questionable whether or not it was a part of the original text—is the

account of the woman who was taken in adultery. It is found only in certain manuscripts of the New Testament. The woman was caught in the act, it seems, and brought before Jesus by the scribes and Pharisees for a reason that appeared good to them at the time. They wanted to test his attitude toward the Old Testament law. The law plainly said that the penalty in such a case was death. Jesus bent down and scribbled something in the sand.
John Then he stood up and said, "Let him who is
8:1–11 without sin among you be the first to throw a
stone at her." Gradually, one by one, all the accusers vanished. Then Jesus looked at the accused and said, "Woman, where are they? Has no one accused you?" She said, "No one." Then Jesus said, "Neither do I condemn you; go, and do not sin again."

The Apostle Paul seldom missed an oppor-
Gal. tunity to cry out against both adultery and
5:19 fornication, nor did he hesitate to add that
Col. "those who do such things shall not inherit the
3:5 kingdom of God." The *Revised Standard*
Eph. *Version* usually has "immorality" for one or
5:3 the other of these two words. But we can be
sure that Paul intended it to cover any and every kind of sexual relation that might conceivably take place outside the state of matrimony.

7

SEDUCTION AND RAPE

THESE TWO categories are discussed together because at times there seems to be a very thin line of distinction between them. Sexual intercourse cannot take place unless the man is sexually aroused. But if the woman has to be enticed to engage in the sexual act, it is seduction. If the man uses force, it is rape. Women may seduce men, or try to, but they cannot rape them. In any event there are examples of all these things in the Bible.

The Deuteronomic legislation has a very involved statement on the seduction of a betrothed virgin which may or may not constitute rape. It all depended. If the alleged act took place in the city the woman had to cry out and scream for help. The cities in ancient times were very compactly built, and the assumption evidently was that someone would hear her and come to her rescue. And if she did not cry out, the presumption was that she was willing. Then if they were caught, both were to be stoned. Her complicity was her guilt, whereas the man was guilty because he

Deut. 22:23–24

had violated the rights of another man—the girl's betrothed.

But if the same act took place in the open country where there was no one to hear her
Deut. screams, then only the man—if they were
22:25–27 caught—was liable for the death sentence. Her guilt could not be proven. She was innocent. But what if she really was guilty, having used her charms to seduce a man who simply did not have the will power to resist? She was still innocent because they did not really know all of this. But what they did know was that he was guilty because he did not resist. He had violated the rights of another man, really of several men—the girl's betrothed, and her father, brothers, or possibly other guardians, who had expected to have received some payment for this girl. But now that she had been violated they could receive nothing. Furthermore, their honor had been offended as well.

Again, if a man raped a virgin who was not
Deut. betrothed to anyone else and he was caught,
22:28–29 he was not put to death but had to marry the girl and pay to her father an indemnity of fifty shekels of silver.

The first rape in the Bible is that of Dinah, daughter of Jacob, in the book of Genesis. It happened in this way. Dinah and her mother Leah went out to visit the women of the land, the Hivites of Shechem. There, Shechem, son
Gen. of Hamor the prince of that land, saw her. "He
34 seized her, lay with her and humbled her."

Evidently pleased with his victim, the prince now wanted to marry the girl. He said to his father, "Get me this maiden [although she was no longer a maiden] for my wife."

The problem was that he had taken the girl before any kind of an approach to her family had been made. When Simeon and Levi, the girl's full brothers, heard of it they were furious and plotted revenge. They asked the Shechemites if they would all be circumcised as a part of the marriage agreement. Then, when the Shechemites were all sore "on the third day," the two brothers rushed in and slaughtered the entire male population of the town. When Jacob heard what had happened he was naturally quite disturbed, but there was not much he could do about it at that point. He did speak to Simeon and Levi but they said, "Should he treat our sister as a harlot?"

One of the most interesting little stories in the Bible is that of a woman trying to seduce a man. The woman was the wife of Potiphar, a captain of Pharaoh's guard, and the man was Joseph, who at the time was the chief steward in the household. This was of course before Joseph's rise to fame and riches. The woman is unnamed, but many a seminarian has had to remember her simply as Potiphar's wife. Actually, it is the Egyptian "Tale of Two Brothers," still extant, or the Greek myth of "Hippolytus and Phaedra." This is the Biblical version. No clearer picture of attempted seduction was ever presented than in the identi-

cal plots of these three stories. Perhaps we should call it: "attempt to vamp." For, alas, the poor woman never succeeded, although she surely tried hard enough. Day after day, when
Gen. her husband was out, she said to Joseph, "Lie
39:6–20 with me. Lie with me." One day she literally pulled his clothes off him and still was refused. For the proud wife, this was more than she could bear, especially from a servant. So she yelled out to the other servants, and later to her husband, that Joseph had actually tried to rape her. As a result Joseph was thrown into prison, thus bringing to an end this particular phase of his dramatic career. But one suspects that the seemingly enraged husband did not entirely believe his wife's story. For if he had, the code of the day would have required that he do away with Joseph right then and there.

The most shocking story of rape in the entire Bible—in fact, one of the most lurid episodes in all literature—is the story in the final chapters of Judges about the rape and dismemberment of a poor concubine. It happened in this way. A man and his concubine were traveling through the territory of Benjamin on their way to the hill country of Ephraim. Evening came and they had to pass the night, so they turned in to the village of Gibeah. There they were about to bed down in the town square when an old man came and persuaded them to spend the night in his house. So they went. What happened after this had best be told in the words of the text itself.

As they were making their hearts merry, behold, the men of the city, base fellows, beset the house round about, beating on the door; and they said to the old man, "Bring out the man who came into your house, that we may know him." And the man, the master of the house, went out to them and said to them, "No, my brethren, do not act so wickedly; seeing that this man has come into my house, do not do this vile thing. Behold, here are my virgin daughter and his concubine; let me bring them out now. Ravish them and do with them what seems good to you; but against this man do not do so vile a thing." But the men would not listen to him. So the man seized his concubine, and put her out to them; and they knew her, and abused her all night until the morning. And as the dawn began to break, they let her go. And as morning appeared, the woman came and fell down at the door of the man's house where her master was, till it was light.

Judg. 19:22–30

And her master rose up in the morning, and when he opened the doors of the house and went out to go on his way, behold there was his concubine lying at the door of the house, with her hands on the threshold. He said to her, "Get up, let us be going." But there was no answer. Then he put her upon the ass; and the man rose up and went away to his home. And when he entered his house, he took a knife, and laying hold of his con-

> cubine he divided her, limb by limb, into twelve pieces, and sent her throughout all the territory of Israel. And all who saw it said, "Such a thing has never happened or been seen from the day that the people of Israel came up out of the land of Egypt until this day; consider it, take counsel, and speak."

What followed next was a bloody civil war. Concerning the incident itself, many have complained that the action of the host here indicated a total disregard for the importance of females as persons, for he offered the concubine, as well as his virgin daughter, in place of the man. But this was not the main point, which was that to have handed over the man would have been a breach of Oriental hospitality, a serious thing indeed in the ancient Near East. But, then again, any way you look at it, rape is total disregard for the other as a person.

We have already mentioned—under the category of "Consanguinity and Incest"—the rape of David's daughter Tamar by her half-brother Amnon. One hesitates to say which is the more shocking factor here, the incest or the rape. Had both of the characters in the relationship been willing, it would certainly have been the former. But one had to be forced; therefore the element of rape is paramount. Anyway, the girl said to her brother, "No, my brother, do not force me; for such a thing is not done in Israel; . . . speak to the king; for

he will not withhold me from you." This leads us to believe that a marriage between a brother and sister was possible at this stage of Israel's history, or possibly because they were royalty, perhaps because they were only half-brother and half-sister. We will never really know. But what we do know is that in this case "he would
II Sam. 13:1–19 not listen to her; and being stronger than she, he forced her, and lay with her.

"Then Amnon hated her with very great hatred; so that the hatred with which he hated her was greater than the love with which he had loved her." An amazing sentence—after which, he threw her out. Amnon proved himself to be not only the spoiled son of an overly indulgent father, but also completely immature. He later paid for his arrogance with his life at the hands of Tamar's full brother, Absalom.

Our final story in this chapter is from the apocryphal book of Susanna. There we have
Sus. 19–21 the account of two wicked old men who tried to seduce the beautiful Susanna, wife of another. When she adamantly refused their advances they both accused her of adultery in her garden with an imaginary accomplice. Since they were two witnesses against one, Susanna was condemned. But as she was about to be led away to be stoned, the wise young Daniel came to her rescue. Demanding a retrial, he questioned the two witnesses separately and found their testimony in total disagreement. Hence Susanna was exonerated and the two elders were condemned.

8

PROSTITUTION: FEMALE AND MALE

THERE IS no need to define "prostitute." Everyone knows what it means. Occasionally the *Revised Standard Version* of the Bible uses the word. But far more often it uses the plain word "harlot," as does the old *King James*. So shall we, most of the time. Harlots are present in the Bible from Genesis to Revelation. Hence, as the saying goes, it is an old profession.

Starting with the book of Genesis, we have already mentioned the remark of Simeon and Levi after they had massacred the entire adult male population of Shechem simply because one of the Shechemites had seized and violated
Gen. their sister. They said, "Should he treat our
34:31 sister as a harlot?" We might deduce from that, that had their sister been a harlot then it would have been all right to seize and abuse her. This is the first occurrence of the word.

The next one is just a few chapters further down in the same book. When Tamar the daughter-in-law of Judah decided to trick her father-in-law into sleeping with her, the

only way was to disguise herself as a harlot (a particular dress?), station herself by the side of the road, and hope to entice him. Under ordinary circumstances the laws of propriety (and later legislation) forbade him to approach her. The trick worked and Tamar accomplished her real objective, which was to become pregnant by one in the same family as that of her deceased husband. Judah, of course, did not know that it was his daughter-in-law, and never would have if she had not extracted from him some pledges that could later be used as proof. About three months afterwards Judah was told, "Tamar your daughter-in-law has played the harlot; and moreover she is with
Gen. child by harlotry." Judah replied, "Bring her
38:12–30 out, and let her be burned." Then Tamar showed him the pledges, whereupon Judah forgave her and even acknowledged the child-to-be as his own. The son born of this union was not only the ancestor of all the Jews but also of Jesus Christ. We all have some skeletons in our family closets if you go back far enough—and sometimes you don't have to go back very far at all.

It is the consanguinity laws that appear later in Leviticus that forbid sex between a man and his daughter-in-law. The same legis-
Lev. lation commands that you "do not profane
19:29 your daughter by making her a harlot . . ."
Lev. Again, it says that if the daughter of a priest
21:9 plays the harlot, she shall be burned. The Deuteronomic legislation says, "There shall be

no cult prostitute of the daughters of Israel,
Deut. 23:17 neither shall there be a cult prostitute of the sons of Israel."

This brings us to one of the most difficult problems of the entire Bible to discuss intelligently and try to understand. It is the problem of the so-called "cult prostitute" of Old Testament times. We simply do not know enough about how the system worked. First of all, for us there is the difficulty of visualizing anyone having sex in church and calling it a religious act. But the Old Testament is full of references to it. The Canaanite cult, which surrounded ancient Israel, had observed the custom for centuries, perhaps similarly to the way in which it was observed in Babylonia, as the religions of the two countries were strikingly alike in other respects. From Book One of Herodotus' *The Histories* we have the following account that might prove of interest:

> There is one custom amongst these people which is wholly shameful: every woman who is a native of the country must once in her life go and sit in the temple of Aphrodite and there give herself to a strange man. Many of the rich women, who are too proud to mix with the rest, drive to the temple in covered carriages with a whole host of servants following behind, and there wait; most, however, sit in the precinct of the temple with a band of plaited string around their

> heads—and a great crowd they are, what with some sitting there, others arriving, others going away—and through them all, gangways are marked off running in every direction for the men to pass along and make their choice. Once a woman has taken her seat she is not allowed to go home until a man has thrown a silver coin into her lap and taken her outside to lie with her. As he throws the coin, the man has to say, "In the name of the goddess Mylitta"—that being the Assyrian name for Aphrodite. The value of the coin is of no consequence; once thrown it becomes sacred, and the law forbids that it should ever be refused. The woman has no privilege of choice—she must go with the first man who throws her the money. When she has lain with him, her duty to the goddess is discharged and she may go home, after which it will be impossible to seduce her by any offer, however large. Tall, handsome women soon manage to get home again, but the ugly ones stay a long time before they can fulfil the condition which the law demands, some of them, indeed, as much as three or four years. There is a custom similar to this in parts of Cyprus.*

The reference to going "outside" would allude to the sacred grove that surrounded

*Herodotus, *The Histories*, translated by Aubrey de Sélincourt (Penguin Books, 1954), pp. 94–95.

the temples or was nearby. These, too, are mentioned by Old Testament writers, particularly the prophets, and they invariably inveigh against them. The whole thing supposedly had to do with insuring the fertility of the soil for another year. But this being the case, what would male cult prostitutes have to do?

Here we come to an even more puzzling problem than that of the female cult prostitute. Just what did the male cult prostitutes do? Did they engage in heterosexual relations with female clients or homosexual relations with visiting male clients? On the basis of one
Deut. 23:17–18 reference in the Deuteronomic law, it was the latter. For there the female cult prostitute is likened to a harlot and the male cult prostitute to a "dog," which, according to the learned footnotes in the *Revised Standard Version,* was a euphemism for "sodomite."

The cult prostitutes were at one time instituted as a part of the worship within the precincts of the temple in Jerusalem. But, according to the Biblical historians themselves (authors of I and II Kings), it was always during a period of apostasy. We are told that
I Kgs. 14:24 there were "male cult prostitutes in the land" as far back as the days of Rehoboam, son of
I Kgs. 15:12 Solomon, but that Solomon's great-grandson Asa put them "out of the land." Still, 175 years later the good king Josiah had to break down
II Kgs. 23:7 "the houses of the male cult prostitutes which were in the house of the LORD." This means in the temple or temple area.

The most famous of all "scarlet women" of
the Bible was the harlot Rahab of Jericho, who
harbored the two spies sent out by Joshua to
Josh. make a report on Palestine just before the
2 invading armies went in. We are told that they
came "into the house of a harlot whose name
was Rahab, and lodged there." As the story
goes, they were dislodged, or forced to flee,
before the night was over by the king's soldiers
who had been sent to capture them. Therefore
we have no way of knowing whether or not
they had time enough to complete what one
usually does when going to the houses of
Josh. harlots. But we do know that they told Rahab
2:21 to put a "scarlet cord in the window" in order
6:25 that she (and her relatives) might be spared on
the day of Jericho's fall. She did so and was
spared. One would have to try hard to find an
Heb. earlier reference than this to the red light in
11:31 the window. Incidentally, pious New Testa-
Jas. ment writers have commended Rahab for her
2:25 saving of the spies—but not for her harlotry.

Judg. Jephthah, one of the judges of Israel, was the
11:1 son of a harlot. Another one, Samson, saw a
16:1 harlot at Gaza and "went in to her." The
prophet Amos rebuked the men of Samaria
Amos because both they and their sons went in to the
2:7 same prostitute. The prophet Joel castigated
those nations that had conquered Jerusalem,
Joel for he said that they had, among other crimes,
3:3 even made boys there into harlots!

The Old Testament prophets in general were constantly comparing Israel's conduct with

harlotry. These references have generally been
interpreted to mean the worship of foreign
Jer. gods, or "playing the harlot" with the faith,
2:20 so to speak. Jeremiah described these harlotries
3:6 as taking place "on every high hill and under
every green tree." Because those were precisely
the places in which the Canaanite cult prostitutes
functioned, we suspect that these acts
were more real than imagined. Ezekiel described
Israel's prostitution of itself with
Ezek. foreign "lovers" even more vividly than
16 Jeremiah had done. No one, however, re-
23 acted more dramatically to the situation than
Hosea. Supposedly in order to point up to the
Hos. nation what it had done, he married a "wife
1:2 of harlotry." Later *she* (the harlot) was rather
cryptically identified with Israel (*herself*). Thus,
maybe he didn't marry a harlot at all: it was
just a figure of speech, the critics say. But he
plainly says that he did marry one.

When we come to the New Testament,
harlots are still with us. Mary Magdalene, one
of Jesus' closest associates, was reputedly a
scarlet woman, although we are never specifically
told that she was. We are told that Jesus
Luke had cast out of her seven demons and that she
8:2 had been healed of evil spirits. But in addition
to this, she has often been identified with the
woman of questionable reputation who anointed
Jesus at the dinner party of Simon the
Pharisee. While this dramatic act was taking
place, Simon was musing to himself, "If this
man were a prophet, he would have known

Luke who and what sort of woman this is who is
7:36–50 touching him, for she is a sinner." Luke himself, in introducing her to the reader, had already called her "a woman of the city." Again, Mary Magdalene has been identified
John with the unnamed woman taken in adultery
8:1–11 described in John's Gospel. Harlot or not, Jesus not only did not hesitate to associate with her but she became one of the most important of all witnesses to the resurrection on that first Easter day.

Jesus never had anything negative to say about harlots. In fact, once in a heated discussion with the chief priests and elders of the
Matt. people he told them that "the tax collectors
21:31 and the harlots will go into the kingdom of God before you." He refers to them in the best loved of all parables, that of the Prodigal Son. Near the end of the story the elder brother
Luke says to the father, "But when this son of yours
15:30 came, who has devoured your living with harlots, you killed for him the fatted calf!" He is referring of course to his younger brother who, in spite of what he had done, was restored completely to the father's love.

The Apostle Paul is almost mute on the subject of harlots in comparison with his interest in other lively subjects. In his writings there are only two occurrences of the word. Together they constitute only one reference, and it is derogatory. He wrote:

> Do you know that your bodies are members

> of Christ? Shall I therefore take the members of Christ and make them members of a
> *I Cor. 6:15–16* prostitute? Never! Do you not know that he who joins himself to a prostitute becomes one body with her? For it is written, "The two shall become one."

His conclusion: avoid any appearances of what he calls "immorality."

The Revelation of St. John the Divine, the last book of the Bible, uses the figure of the harlot to personify one of its most brilliant images, "the city which has dominion over the kings of the earth," and with which "the kings of the earth have committed fornication." The author calls her (the city) "the great harlot who
Rev. 17 is seated upon many waters"—obviously Rome of the seven hills. An entire chapter is devoted to the description.

So, as we have said, from Genesis to Revelation we encounter harlotry. But should anything that has been so commonplace in the history of the world be out of place in the Bible? Obviously it is not.

9

BESTIALITY

BESTIALITY is defined as "sexual relations between a human being and a lower animal."* According to the late Dr. Kinsey, this is something that if found at all is most likely to be found among farm boys. Palestine in Biblical times was an agricultural country, and the evidence indicates that the people were more than casually aware of this sexual deviation. We are never told that anyone in the Bible was actually caught in the act of bestiality, but at least four times the law codes mention it, and of course it is expressly forbidden. There would have been no need to forbid it so often unless there had been some actual instances.

First, the Levitical code says that "you shall
Lev. 18:23 not lie with any beast and defile yourself with it, neither shall any woman give herself to any beast to lie with it; it is perversion." Then two
Lev. 20:15–16 chapters later in the same book we read that if either a man or a woman "lies with a beast," the offender shall be put to death—and the unfortunate beast as well. The death penalty

**Webster's*, 1971.

Exod. for this offense had already been stated in the
22:19 book of Exodus, but evidently the compilers of
Leviticus felt called upon to repeat it. But we
have no way of knowing whether or not this
penalty was ever invoked. Finally there is the
List of the Twelve Curses. This ancient list—
and liturgy—describes a number of people who
are to be socially anathema to the whole com-
Deut. munity. Among them is "he who lies with any
27:21 kind of beast." And all the people shall say,
"Amen."

Other than rape, bestiality is the only bit of totally anti-social sexual behavior mentioned in the Bible. There is no reference to necrophilia or to any other extremely anti-social sexual aberration.

There are two references, stated quite casual-
II Kgs. ly, to eating "dung" and drinking urine, but
18:27 they are allusions to the kind of conduct to
Isa. which some people might have to resort in a
36:12 time of protracted siege. They are not associated with any kind of sexual aberration.

There is also a reference to a woman "del-
Deut. icately bred," who will eat "her afterbirth
28:56–57 that comes out from between her feet" (and
her own children). But this too is a reference
to something that might take place only in
time of the most severe siege.

10

EUNUCHS AND TRANSVESTITES

THE DEFINITION of a *eunuch* is "a castrated man placed in charge of a harem or employed as a chamberlain in a palace," or any "man or boy deprived of the testes or external genitals."* But, as the *Encyclopaedia Britannica,* in its article on the subject, reminds us: "The common idea that eunuchs are necessarily deficient in courage and intellectual vigour is amply refuted by history." Certainly many of them attained very high positions in the Middle East. Eunuchs are mentioned in the Bible approximately forty times. We shall name only a few references.

It was "two or three eunuchs" of ancient Israel who were so zealous for the true faith that they threw the apostate Queen Jezebel out the window to her death, thus expressing their solidarity with the religious reformer Jehu. The book of Isaiah says that if eunuchs are true believers then they are not to say, "I am

II Kgs. 9:32–33

* *Webster's*, 1971.

Isa. 56:3–5 a dry tree." God will give to them a reward greater than sons and daughters.

The book of Esther gives us the best Biblical picture of the eunuch as harem-keeper. The setting of the book, however, is not Palestine but Persia. According to the customs of this Eastern court, there was one eunuch who was in charge of the virgins and another in charge of those who had already visited the royal *Esth. 2:13–15* bed. These women of "the second harem," however, could never return to the king's chambers unless personally summoned by him. But we are also told that before each maiden "went in to the king in this way" for the first time she was allowed to take with her whatever she desired from the harem. When Esther's turn came she asked to take with her "nothing except what Hegai the king's eunuch, who had charge of the women, advised." This secret—whatever it was—along with her own natural beauty and talent, enabled Esther to become queen. The story reveals, among other things, that eunuchs certainly knew a great deal about what it took to please the king.

There is a very strange saying of Jesus about eunuchs. It is quoted by Matthew as follows:

> *Matt. 19:12* For there are eunuchs who have been so from birth, and there are eunuchs who have been made eunuchs by men, and there are eunuchs who have made themselves eunuchs for the sake of the kingdom of heaven. He who is able to receive this, let him receive it.

The last part of this saying was taken quite literally in the early days of Christianity by some who went so far as to emasculate themselves voluntarily so as to be no longer troubled by sexual desires, or so they thought anyway. Actually, to be deprived of the testicles does not necessarily indicate that a man will no longer have sexual desire. But perhaps he will not have as much. The most celebrated of these *castrati,* as they were called, was the theologian Origen.

According to the book of Acts, one of the first persons converted when the new Christian faith spread beyond Jerusalem was a eunuch. He was also a black man. Converted by Philip the Deacon, the Ethiopian eunuch was "a minister of Candace the queen of the Ethiopians, in charge of all her treasure," who "had come up to Jerusalem to worship." Hence, on the basis of that statement, before his conversion to Christianity he was most likely a black Jew.

Acts 8:27–39

We do not know that eunuchs dressed any differently from other men who occupied similar positions. Probably they did not. But the preceding survey shows that they were highly regarded by Jews and Christians alike. Not so transvestites. Transvestitism was strictly forbidden by the Deuteronomic code with these words:

A woman shall not wear anything that

> *Deut. 22:5* pertains to a man, nor shall a man put on a woman's garment; for whoever does these is an abomination to the LORD your God.

Of course this assumes that they knew what kind of clothes a man was supposed to wear, and likewise a woman. Obviously this was the case, as some kind of distinction in dress is clearly indicated here.

The question might arise as to whether or not the sexes could be distinguished by the length of their hair, and this is difficult to answer. The only thing we can say is that both
II Sam. 14:26 sexes had long hair in Old Testament times, as in the ancient East generally, although we do not know if both sexes wore their hair equally long. Perhaps the man's hair was a bit shorter and worn with little or no ornamentation in contrast to the woman's, which was somewhat ornamented, as we know from ancient Mesopotamia. In New Testament times there was some distinction in their hair lengths, as indicated by these words that Paul wrote to the church at Corinth:

> *I Cor. 11:14–15* Does not nature itself teach you that for a man to wear long hair is degrading to him, but if a woman has long hair, it is her pride? For her hair is given her for a covering.

Luke 7:38 The woman who anointed Jesus with oil and wiped his feet with her hair must have had hair that reached halfway down her back or longer; otherwise she would not in this case have been able to use her hair for a towel. If this were true of most women, then men could have had shoulder-length hair and still have been quite distinguishable from the opposite sex, where hair was concerned.

In any event, whatever the outward distinctions between the sexes might have been, in both the Old Testament and the New there are outbursts against the man who appears to be "effeminate." King David identified such
II Sam. behavior—or predisposition, as the case may
3:29 be—as nothing less than a curse (see next
chapter), which was a terrible thing in the Old
I Cor. Testament; and Paul the Apostle went so far
6:9–10 as to say that the "effeminate" (man) would
never inherit the kingdom of heaven. But this brings us to a new topic.

11

HOMOSEXUALITY

HOMOSEXUALITY, according to the *Encyclopaedia Britannica,* refers to "sexual attraction of a person to one of the same sex (from Gr[eek] *homo-*, 'same'; not from Lat[in] *homo*, 'human being', 'man')." Nevertheless, the references to homosexuality in the Bible—with one possible exception—refer to male homosexuality. There is possibly one reference to female homosexuality or lesbianism. We shall take it up at the end of this chapter.

The first book in the Bible contains one of the most blatant stories of homosexuality ever told. In fact, it contributes a name that has so often been identified with all male homosexuality. The word is *sodomy,* and the story is that of Lot in Sodom. We will try to present the gist of the story, plus some background.

Abraham and his nephew Lot together with their respective families at first lived in close proximity. But the two men had a misunderstanding and they decided to separate. While Abraham continued to live in tents, thus maintaining the desert purity of his ancestors, Lot decided to move into a town called Sodom. Very shortly, we are told, "the outcry" against the city was great, reaching apparently up to heaven.

One evening while Lot was sitting by the town gate two angels approached—in disguise of course. Lot extended to them an invitation to partake of the hospitality of his home, which they accepted. While Lot prepared food for them, the news of their arrival spread through the town, and before they could retire for the evening,

> the men of the city, the men of Sodom, both young and old, all the people to the last man, surrounded the house; and they called to Lot, "Where are the men who came to you tonight? Bring them out to us that we may know them." Lot went out . . . and said, 'I beg you, my brothers, do not act so wickedly. Behold, I have two daughters who have not known man; let me bring them out to you, and do to them as you please; only do nothing to these men, for they have come under the shelter of my roof." Then the Sodomites said, "Stand back! This fellow came to sojourn and he would play the judge! Now we will deal worse with you than with them."

Gen. 19:4–9

Then they drew near to break down the door. At that point the two angels pulled Lot in and bolted the door, but not until they had struck blind all those who were standing outside. Then the angels instructed Lot and his family to quit the city promptly, for at any moment it would be totally destroyed. They told them that not under any conditions were they to look back. Lot's wife did look, and she became a pillar of salt. This was a good way to explain the human-like salt figures found later along the shores of the Dead Sea where Sodom once stood. Some Biblical critics have said that the cities of Sodom and Gomorrah (also said to have been destroyed for its wickedness) might have collapsed completely into the sea, or might have died because of the gradual build-up of salt there. But the text of the Bible simply states that there "rained on Sodom and Gomorrah brimstone and fire from the LORD out of heaven." They have been legend ever since. But even more legendary has been the behavior of the Sodomites—a behavior that to this day has been called by the name of sodomy.

Just what is sodomy? The book of Genesis, in the chapters up to this point, has many times used the verb "to know" to mean sexual intercourse between man and woman. In this
Gen. story the men of Sodom say, "Where are the
19:5 men who came to you tonight? Bring them out
that we might *know* them." Sodomy then would be anal intercourse.

The story is unusually sordid. But by way of explanation we should add that the Israelites seldom missed an opportunity to point up the decadence of the Canaanite civilization, which was in Palestine when they arrived but which they fully intended to displace. The Canaanite civilization—which included Sodom and many other cities—had assuredly been there for seven or eight hundred years by the time the Israelites arrived, and it had indeed become corrupt, as civilizations have the tendency to do. In this story flagrant homosexuality is presented as an indication of that corruption. But lest anyone think that homosexuality in the Bible was confined strictly to the Canaanites, let us now turn to an equally flagrant case of Israelite homosexuality, or bisexuality as the case may be.

This is the rather gory account of the Ephraimite and his concubine who were passing through the territory of Benjamin and had to spend the night in the little town of
Judg. 19 Gibeah. The story is found near the end of the
book of Judges, and it has already been presented in some detail in chapter seven. So similar is the general outline of this story to that of Lot in Sodom that it seems likely that the first one was used as a literary model for the second. This time, however, the men do accept the woman who is offered them, although they would have preferred the man. This, then, would indicate the acceptance of bisexuality in this Israelite tribe rather than homosexuality, strictly speaking. Their treatment of the woman, however, was subhuman, and in the first story the very idea of Lot's offering his virgin daughters in place of

the honored guests is beyond our comprehension. Such, however, were the mores of the Middle East at the time.

Some of the critics have said that the second story was freely composed by members of King David's court for the purpose of smearing Gibeah, which had been the home town of Saul, Israel's previous king. The suggestion is interesting, but whether true or not the story does point up that Israelite writers could just as easily visualize homosexuality—formerly the Canaanite vice—among themselves as among others.

The only example in the Old Testament of an unabashed homosexual love of one well-known character for another is the story of the undying friendship between David and Jonathan. Of course there are those who say that it was just that—friendship and nothing more. Let us look at what material there is.

We are told that after David was introduced
to the army of Saul, "the soul of Jonathan
I Sam. [Saul's son] was knit to the soul of David,
18:1–3 and Jonathan loved him as his own soul. . . .
Then Jonathan made a covenant with David,
because he loved him as his own soul." Next
we learn that Jonathan stripped off his own
clothes and armor and gave them to David.

That Saul knew about his son's preference
for David is revealed in the following remark
he made to Jonathan: "You son of a perverse,
I Sam. rebellious woman, do I not know that you have
20:30 chosen the son of Jesse [David] to your own

shame, and to the shame of your mother's nakedness?" If we compare this to the reference to uncovering the father's nakedness in Genesis 9:20–25—a veiled reference to the usual Canaanite debauchery—then we see it as a clear reference to a sexual relationship.

When Saul announces that he intends to kill
David, the two friends arrange a secret
I Sam. meeting and have quite a tearful farewell. We
20:41 read: "David rose from beside the stone heap
and fell on his face to the ground, and bowed three times; and they kissed one another, and wept with one another, until David recovered himself." They parted, never to meet again.

The final bit of testimony that shows how David felt about Jonathan is contained in the elegy that David sang for both Saul and Jonathan on the occasion of their deaths. The relevant verse is:

I am distressed for you, my brother
  Jonathan;
II Sam. very pleasant have you been to me;
1:26 your love to me was wonderful,
  passing the love of women.

David also showed a fatherly concern for Jonathan's surviving son, Meribaal.

The kind of friendship that David shared with Jonathan has been compared to that of Achilles and Patroclus in the *Iliad*, of Gilgamesh and Enkidu in the *Gilgamesh Epic*, the oldest extant epic poem of ancient Babylonia, and of Alexander the Great and Hephaestion in later history.* This is to say that such men were far from being effeminate in any way; they were warrior friends. They were essentially bisexual men. David, for example, also had eight wives, and the others mentioned above had their fair share of women too.

The following story illustrates that David would have had little time for effeminate men. When his commander Joab assassinated the northern commander Abner, who had come to make peace, David angrily exclaimed:

> I and my kingdom are forever guiltless before the LORD for the blood of Abner the son of Ner. May it fall upon the head of Joab, and upon all his father's house; and may the house of Joab never be without one who has a discharge, or who is leprous, or who holds a spindle, or who is slain by the sword, or who lacks bread!

II Sam. 3:28–29

The reference to one "who holds a spindle" here is an allusion to an effeminate man. In this particularly lusty period of Israel's history real men did not spin or weave.

We have already referred to the male cult prostitutes who were somehow a part of the Canaanite religious cult that surrounded

*Gladys Schmitt has written a novel on the subject of the friendship between David and Jonathan (*David, the King*, Dial Press, 1946); and Mary Renault has retold the friendship between Alexander and Hephaestion (*Fire From Heaven*, Pantheon Books, 1969).

Deut. 23:17–18 Israel. The evidence indicates that the sex that they practiced there was indeed sodomy (see chapter eight: "Prostitution: Female and Male"). What we cannot be sure of is precisely how they functioned in association with the Israelite temple in Jerusalem. We do know that they were there, for we read that the good King Josiah broke down "the houses of the male cult prostitutes which were in the house of the LORD." *II Kgs. 23:7* The Hebrew term for "female cult prostitute" would be *kedeshah*; but the term used here is *kadesh*, or "male cult prostitute." On this subject the *Encyclopaedia Britannica* article, "Homosexuality," has the following to say:

> There is some doubt about the attitude to the homosexual temple prostitute, or *kadesh*, in the earliest period of Judaism, but by the time of the "Holiness code" any form of homosexuality was sternly forbidden among the Jews (Lev. xviii, xx); such practices were regarded as pagan, the way of the Chaldean, of the Canaanite or of the Egyptian, a form of idolatry.

The consensus of scholarship is that the book of Leviticus (containing the "Holiness code" referred to above) was not written by Moses—indeed, the question is if any of the laws were—but appeared sometime after the period of the Israelite kings; more specifically, about the time of the Jewish exile in Babylonia. Hence,

when the male cult prostitutes were attached to the temple at Jerusalem, as well as in the earlier period of David, the book of Leviticus, which contains the famed prohibitions, did not
Lev. 20:13 exist. A later chapter of this code will say that male homosexuality should be punishable by death. But we have no way of knowing whether or not this penalty was ever carried out.

The Levitical prohibition of homosexuality was introduced into Christianity by Paul of Tarsus, ever zealous for strict observances of sexual purity. In one of his earliest pieces of correspondence he reminds the Corinthians
I Cor. 6:9–10 that "neither the immoral, nor idolaters, nor adulterers, nor homosexuals . . . will inherit the kingdom of God." The *Revised Standard Version* that we have quoted here has a footnote that says: "Two Greek words are rendered by this expression"—that is, *homosexuals.* The *King James Version* keeps both words and renders them: "effeminate" (males) and "abusers of themselves with mankind." The two Greek words in question are *malakoi* and *arsenokoitai.** The first of these actually referred to "catamites," or extremely effeminate young men or boys who were homosexual, while the second was understood to mean "pederasts" or "sodomites." *Paiderastia* (pederasty) in ancient Greece had to do with the sexual

*Readers are advised to consult various translations of the Bible in order to compare the variety of ways in which these two words have been rendered.

attraction of older men to teen-aged boys, and such practices were common. Certainly all males who engage in homosexuality do not fall under the category of either the catamite or the pederast; neither can all homosexual activity be classified, according to the Biblical understanding of the word, as "sodomy."

The above definition of terms is not meant to be an attempt to say that Paul would not have put all homosexual behavior under his disapprobation. But every Biblical passage must be seen against its background. No place in the ancient world, except possibly Pompeii, was more widely known for its licentiousness than was Corinth. It was, so to speak, the "sin city" or "sex capital" of Greece at the time; and it was to the Corinthian church that Paul
I Cor. was writing this letter. His next statement to
6:11 the Corinthians was: "And such were some of you." He meant that before their conversion some of them were given over to such things. But now that they were members of the church better things were expected of them! Paul, if
I Cor. he could, would have substituted continence
7:1 for sexuality in any case (Had he not said, "It is well for a man not to touch a woman"?); but this would certainly have been true in the cases of those vices that he particularly associated with the pagan world. Homosexuality was one of the chief among them.

I Tim. The first letter to Timothy, which may or
1:10 may not have been written by Paul, mentions "sodomites" (*arsenokoitai*) among a long list

of "immoral persons" for whom the Old Testament law was given in the first place. The author does not mention here that earlier the magnificent Epistle to the Galatians had disavowed the importance of this law.

Finally, male and possibly female homosexuality are referred to by Paul in the opening chapter of his sermon-letter to the infant church at Rome. He is speaking of the conduct of peoples past and present throughout the world and of the kinds of behavior in which God allowed them to engage while they were still in error; for example:

> Their women exchanged natural relations for unnatural, and the men likewise gave up natural relations with women and were consumed with passion for one another, men committing shameless acts with men and receiving in their own persons the due penalty for their error.

Rom. 1:26–27

The opening words of this quotation may refer to female homosexuality, but not necessarily. Anal intercourse with the female is another possibility. But we know from other sources that lesbianism was widely practiced in ancient Rome, the city to which this letter was addressed, and that it was much more prevalent there than in ancient Greece. Furthermore, the use of the word "likewise" and a comparison with the remainder of the sentence makes us suspect that it is a reference to lesbian behavior; and, if it is, it has the distinction of being the only such reference in Scripture.

Unlike Paul, Jesus Christ never said anything about homosexuality—one way or the other.

12

MASTURBATION AND *COITUS INTERRUPTUS*

Because of one troublesome word in the English language, two entirely different sexual acts are often confused in point of reference. The word is "onanism." Is onanism masturbation or uncompleted intercourse? *Webster's Seventh* gives both of these definitions of onanism, but in the reverse order. However, when the word is used in our sexual manuals, usually it is masturbation that is meant. But onanism in the Bible itself is not exactly masturbation.

Onan "spilled the semen upon the ground," and for centuries onanism has been identified with masturbation. Of course when a man or boy masturbates, that *is* essentially what happens. Hence there is some justification for the definition. But Onan himself did not masturbate. Masturbation involves primarily manual stimulation of the genital organs in order to achieve orgasm, and that is not what Onan did. He actually had intercourse, but it was an uncompleted intercourse. For before experiencing orgasm he withdrew from the woman and then "spilled the semen on the ground." Some books call such behavior *coitus interruptus*, and that is what should be understood by onanism—after Onan, son of Judah, whose story is recorded in the first book of the Bible.

The background of the story is that Onan's older brother Er had died without offspring. Therefore the old custom of levirate marriage demanded that the next brother perform the duty of a husband for his brother's widow, that he might produce offspring and perpetuate a name for his deceased brother. But, we are told:

> *Gen. 38:9–10* Onan knew that the offspring would not be his; so when he went in to his brother's wife he spilled the semen on the ground, lest he should give offspring to his brother. And what he did was displeasing in the sight of the LORD, and he slew him . . .

This is not a reference to masturbation. But by interpreting it as such, moralists of the past could use this text as a deterrent to a sexual practice of which they did not approve.

But there is one passage in the Bible that seems certain to be a reference to masturbation, and possibly there are three. In the Levitical code we read:

> And if a man has an emission of semen, he

> shall bathe his whole body in water, and be
> *Lev. 15:16–17* unclean until the evening. And every garment and every skin on which the semen comes shall be washed with water, and be unclean until the evening.

When a man has intercourse the semen is deposited elsewhere, not in his garments. Of course there is such a thing as an emission in sleep when the garments might again be involved (to be discussed in the next chapter). But there is no mention of sleep here. Masturbation seems to be the meaning. Incidentally the uncleanness referred to in this case is a ritual impurity as well as an actual uncleanness.

Further down in the same code we have another possible reference to masturbation. We
Lev. 22:4 read that anyone who so much as touches "a man who has had an emission of semen" is ritually unclean until the evening. This "emission of semen" could refer to masturbation, intercourse, or even to an involuntary emission.

The other possible reference to masturbation is in David's curse upon Joab when he becomes angry with his unruly commander. He says, "May the house of Joab never be without
II Sam. 3:29 one who has a discharge, or who is leprous, or who holds a spindle" and so on. One major scholar, R. H. Pfeiffer,* has translated the phrase "one who holds a spindle" here as

*R. H. Pfeiffer, *The Hebrew Iliad* (Harper & Brothers, 1957), p. 75.

"masturbator." But the idea of an effeminate man (one who holds a spindle) is much more in keeping with the particular sense of the curse.

Furthermore, on the basis of what we have found in this survey, the Bible never has anything negative to say about masturbation. *Coitus interruptus,* however, on the basis of what happened to Onan, is quite a bad thing.

13

NOCTURNAL EMISSIONS

WHEN A MAN has an involuntary ejaculation of semen it is usually accompanied by a dream and takes place at night or in the morning during or immediately following upon a deep sleep; hence the expression "nocturnal emission." It is also referred to as "emission in sleep." This experience, which practically every young man knows about or should, is clearly alluded to in the Deuteronomic code as follows:

> If there is among you any man who is not clean by reason of what chances to him by night, then he shall go outside the camp he shall not come within the camp; but when evening comes on, he shall bathe himself in water, and when the sun is down, he may come within the camp.

Deut. 23:10–11

The words in the original Hebrew are even clearer here. The reference is to something over which the man has absolutely no control. It is a nocturnal emission.

In our discussion of masturbation in the previous chapter, we mentioned a passage in Leviticus that speaks rather ambiguously *Lev. 22:4* about "a man who has had an emission of semen." This could possibly be a reference to a nocturnal emission. In any event he would be ritually unclean. Ritual uncleanness is also the real subject of the clear-cut reference to nocturnal emissions from Deuteronomy quoted above.

Ritual cleanness or uncleanness is one of the major concerns of the book of Leviticus and occasionally it turns up in Deuteronomy, I Samuel, and elsewhere. The subject will also recur in our next chapter, on "Menstruation," and in the chapter after that, on "Venereal Diseases." Therefore, perhaps we should say just a word about what is meant by it. Ritual uncleanness implies that one cannot participate in the religious life of the community or in any community activities, including attendance at public gatherings, until the condition is removed. Actually the religious life of the community and its social or public life were one and the same. The Bible does not separate religion from life as we do. This we might consider to be quite a natural thing after we stop to think about it. But what we do not pause to consider, until we are confronted with all of this material, is the close association between religion and sex.

Most of the time, it seems, ritual uncleanness has to do one way or the other with sex. In the

same passage mentioned above, which refers to "a man who has had an emission of semen,"
Lev. there is the statement that a priest or Levite
22:4 who "suffers a discharge" may not eat of the holy things. Again, religion and sex. But this is not a reference to a nocturnal emission. It is a reference to some kind of venereal disease, a topic that will be dealt with in a coming chapter. First, however, a digression on menstruation.

14

MENSTRUATION

IN THE PRECEDING chapter we discussed a natural experience to which healthy males are subject, at least so long as they are in their prime. Now let us turn to the female and the Biblical view of menstruation: not only was it "the way of women," it was "the time of her impurity."

Gen. 31:35

Here we note the prevailing attitude toward menstruation in the Old Testament—it was considered to be a period of impurity for the woman. During this period the woman was unclean both physically and ritually. We have already mentioned ritual impurity and the fact that certain penalties were associated with it, as well as certain requirements that had to be met before one was clean again.

Lev. 15:25

The Levitical code states:

> When a woman has a discharge of blood which is her regular discharge from her body, she shall be in her impurity for seven days, and whoever touches her shall be unclean until the evening. And everything upon

Lev. 15:19–20

> which she lies during her impurity shall be unclean; everything also upon which she sits shall be unclean. . . .

The passage goes on to say what shall be unclean in regard to all her contacts and what should be done about them. The final verse of the paragraph is the most interesting:

> And if any man lies with her, and her
> *Lev.* impurity is on him, he shall be unclean seven
> *15:24* days; and every bed upon which he lies shall
> be unclean.

This clearly indicates that sexual relations
Lev. sometimes continued during the period,
18:19 although elsewhere in the same law it says that
such relations were strictly prohibited. In fact,
if a man approached a woman during the time
of her uncleanness and they had relations, then
Lev. both of them were to be excommunicated
20:18 ("cut off from among their people").

All of this seems connected to a primitive taboo having to do with menstruation, as is revealed in one of the central chapters of Genesis. When Jacob and his family were fleeing from his father-in-law Laban, they were eventually overtaken as they pitched camp one night. Laban searched through all of Jacob's possessions looking for stolen goods. Actually Jacob's wife Rachel had stolen the household gods—or religious figurines—from her father's home and was sitting upon them in her tent.

She remained seated when her father entered,
saying, "Let not my lord be angry that I cannot
rise before you, for the way of women is upon
me." He searched but found nothing, which
means that he did not go near Rachel. Had he
Gen. done so, he would have found the objects. He
31:35 avoided her because she was menstruating
and was therefore taboo.

The few references that we have to menstru-
Isa. ation in the Old Testament readily identify it
30:22 with whatever is unclean. Once it is simply
Lam. translated "a filthy thing." Even in the apocry-
1:17 phal book of Additions to Esther, when the
Add. Esth. Jewish queen of Persia wanted to speak
14:16 disparagingly of her royal crown, she compared
it to a "menstrual rag."

The only reference to a woman's discharge of
Matt. blood in the New Testament is a very special
9:20 case. It is the story of Christ's healing the
woman "who had had a flow of blood for
Luke twelve years." This could be an abnormal
8:43 menstrual condition or perhaps something
closely associated with it. If it were a ma-
lignancy, it is doubtful that she would have
lived with it for as long as twelve years. Each of
the first three gospels records this story, but
Mark only Mark adds that she "had suffered much
5:26 under many physicians." By touching only the
robe of Christ she was healed. It is worthy of
note here that Jesus did not object to her
touching him: hence he did not consider
menstruation—or whatever her condition was
—as "unclean."

There is in the Old Testament one reference to something that is definitely not menstruation, for it is clearly stated that this particular discharge takes place "not at the time of her impurity":

Lev. 15:25–26

> If a woman has a discharge of blood for many days, not at the time of her impurity, or if she has a discharge beyond the time of her impurity, all the days of the discharge she shall continue in her uncleanness; as in the days of her impurity, she shall be unclean. Every bed on which she lies, all the days of her discharge, shall be to her as the bed of her impurity; and everything on which she sits shall be unclean, as in the uncleanness of her impurity. . . .

Following this we are told what she and those who had come into contact with her had to do in order to become "clean." We can only conjecture what this condition could have been —an abnormal menstruation, a growth of some kind, who knows? It does not sound like a venereal disease; but indications are that the ancient world was not without knowledge of this scourge. To this topic we must now turn.

15

VENEREAL DISEASES

THE PREVAILING point of view is that the peoples of ancient and medieval times knew nothing of venereal diseases until Christopher Columbus discovered America and discovered at the same time, so to speak, the diseases of Venus. But there are many indications that the scourges of both syphilis and gonorrhea were present in the Old World all along. Let us see what the Bible might have to say on the subject.

We have already mentioned (in both chapters eleven and twelve) David's curse upon Joab, in
II Sam. 3:29 which David says: "May the house of Joab never be without one who has a discharge" and so on. A leading Biblical scholar has translated here: "one ill with gonorrhea."* Indeed, we are baffled as to know what else it could be.

Leviticus, chapter fifteen, describes a disease that sounds for all the world like gonorrhea. It reads:

When any man has a discharge from his

*R. H. Pfeiffer, *The Hebrew Iliad* (Harper & Brothers, 1957), p. 75.

> body, his discharge is unclean. And this is the law for his uncleanness for a discharge:
> Lev. 15:2–4 whether his body runs with his discharge, or his body is stopped from discharge, it is uncleanness in him. Every bed on which he who has the discharge lies shall be unclean; and everything on which he sits shall be unclean. . . .

And so it continues, describing regulations that must be observed until the condition clears up and for eight days thereafter. The precise treatment of the malady is not detailed here and we have no way of knowing what it might have been. As noted earlier, Leviticus is primarily interested in what one had to do in order to be ritually clean. Treatment would have been left up to the practitioners, including physicians and pharmacists who were known and respected in Old Testament times.

Gen. 50:2

Ecclus. 38:1–15

But, elsewhere, the Bible describes a disease of a man's "loins"—a euphemism for the genitals and lower abdominal area—for which there seems to have been no cure. The psalmist writes:

> My wounds grow foul and fester
> because of my foolishness,
> I am utterly bowed down and prostrate;
> all the day I go about mourning.
> For my loins are filled with burning,
> and there is no soundness in my flesh.
> I am utterly spent and crushed;

Ps. 38:5–8

> I groan because of the tumult of my heart.

He also says that former friends would not come near him, ending his lament without any indication of a remedy. The description could be that of a syphilitic condition.

So can the following passage from one of the sermons in Deuteronomy:

> The LORD will smite you with the boils of Egypt, and with the ulcers and the scurvy and the itch, of which you cannot be healed. The LORD will smite you with madness and blindness and confusion of mind; and you shall grope at noonday, as the blind grope in darkness . . . and there shall be no one to help you.

Deut. 28:27–29

When God became angry with Miriam she was stricken with leprosy. Then Aaron cried out to Moses on behalf of their stricken sister with these words: "Let her not be as one dead, of whom the flesh is half-consumed when he comes out of his mother's womb." According to the learned authorities on the subject, these words are suggestive of the macerated syphilitic stillborn.*

Num. 12:12

*For this idea and for the general inspiration for this chapter, I am grateful to William Brown *et al.*, *Syphilis and Other Venereal Diseases* (Harvard University Press, 1970) pp. 1–2 and 82. Dr. Brown and his colleagues, in turn, cite as one of the sources of their summary, R. R. Willcox, "Venereal Diseases in the Bible," *British Journal of Venereal Diseases* 25: 28–33 (1949), which lists further bibliography.

And then there was the unnamed disease of the man called Job. It was characterized by
Job "loathesome sores" in the description in the
2:7 prose introduction and described as a source of unceasing pain throughout the long poem. It was finally relieved only because someone has added a "Happy Ending" which most scholars do not consider to have been a part of the original book.

Even the Ten Commandments refer to the
Exod. jealous God who visited the sins of the fathers
20:5 upon the children unto the third and fourth
Deut. generations. Since syphilis is one of the very
5:9 few diseases that is transferred from parent to child at birth, we may have here a veiled reference to this particular form of venereal disease.

Another thing we do not know is whether or not Biblical personages were aware that certain of these afflictions might have come upon them through intercourse. There is a hint of it in Paul's solemn warning to the people of Rome:

> Their women exchanged natural relations for unnatural, and the men likewise gave up natural relations with women and were
> *Rom.* consumed with passion for one another, men
> *1:26–27* committing shameless acts with men and receiving in their own persons the due penalty for their error.

Both syphilis and gonorrhea may be communicated through anal intercourse; and even though they did not know the names of the diseases, they certainly seem to be describing the possibility of their transmission in the last verse of the above passage.

The Bible contains almost everything. Until a few decades ago almost all of it was a mystery to us, and much of it still is. But we press on to know more, regardless of where our search leads us, and we must not be afraid to face what this Book may be trying to tell us of the agelong sufferings of mankind.

16
CIRCUMCISION

CIRCUMCISION, or the cutting away of the foreskin of the penis, is of unknown origin, but it has been practiced by numerous peoples from remotest antiquity. And nowhere does it play a more important role than in the pages of the Bible, in both the Old and New Testaments. It was, and is, a religious rite of first importance to the Jews. In addition to its religious associations it may have been practiced for hygienic reasons; but we are never specifically told this in the Bible.

The ancient Egyptians practiced circumcision, and so did the Western Semites (Israelites, Canaanites, Phoenicians, Arabs, and others). The Eastern Semites (Assyrians and Babylonians) did not, nor did the Greeks or other Aegean peoples. Herodotus has provided us with the following information in regard to the ancient Egyptians: "They practise circumcision, while men of other nations—except those who have learnt from Egypt—leave their private parts as nature made them. . . .They circumcise themselves for cleanliness' sake, preferring to be clean rather than comely."*

Although we may detect a decided Greek prejudice against the rite in the historian's voice here, his words do supply us with the name of one of the most ancient peoples who practiced circumcision and their reason for having done so. But this does not prove that they originated it: perhaps it was (as now) common to various parts of Africa. Nor does Herodotus' writing prove that the Israelites learned of circumcision from Egypt, as has often been suggested. The evidence in regard to the rite in the Bible itself is conflicting, and there is a great deal of which we cannot be certain. But what we do know is that far more importance was attached to the rite after the Jews went into Exile and were living among the uncircumcised Babylonians. Then, for the first time, along with sabbath observance and the dietary laws, it became one of the primary characteristics of the Jew. This is not to say that it had not formerly occupied a prominent place. It assuredly had. But even then circumcision seemed to be much more prominent whenever the Jews came into close contact with peoples who did not practice the rite; for example, with the Philistines, who were of Greek or Aegean descent.

The first account of circumcision in the Old Testament is in the stories of Abraham. It was to be a sign of the covenant between God

*Herodotus, *The Histories*, translated by Aubrey de Sélincourt (Penguin Books, 1954), p. 116.

and Abraham and his descendants. The command is:

> Every male among you shall be circumcised.
> You shall be circumcised in the flesh of your
> foreskins, and it shall be a sign of the
> *Gen.* covenant between me and you. He that is
> *17:10–14* eight days old among you shall be circumcised; every male throughout your generations, whether born in your house, or bought with your money from any foreigner who is not of your offspring, both . . . shall be circumcised. So shall my covenant be in your flesh an everlasting covenant. Any uncircumcised male who is not circumcised in the flesh of his foreskin shall be cut off from his people; he has broken my covenant.

Gen. Later we are told that "Abraham circumcised
21:4 his son Isaac when he was eight days old, as God commanded him."

In the next story involving circumcision there is probably a bit of erroneous reporting. It is the story of the rape of Dinah by the prince of Shechem and the subsequent massacre of the men of Shechem by Dinah's brothers. The brothers massacred the Shechemites "on the
Gen. third day" after their circumcision, which was
34 supposedly required of them in order that the prince might be allowed to marry Dinah. The problem with this is that, so far as we know, the Canaanites had always practiced the rite of circumcision, as did all the Western Semites.

The next account of circumcision is, in a way, another story of the origin of the rite. It has to do with Moses, his wife, and infant son, returning through the desert of Sinai to confront Pharaoh after Moses' encounter with God at the burning bush. We read:

> At a lodging place the LORD met him and sought to kill him. Then Zipporah took a flint and cut off her son's foreskin, and touched Moses' feet with it, and said,
> *Exod.* "Surely you are a bridegroom of blood to
> *4:24–26* me!" So he let him alone. Then it was that she said, "You are a bridegroom of blood," because of the circumcision.

This passage reflects a certain amount of rather primitive Israelite ritual. It has been said that frequently in the Bible the word "feet" is a euphemism for the male sex organs. Later in the same narrative we are told that circumcision is a requirement for admission to the Passover feast. The antiquity of the custom even by this time led to its being stated as an absolute command in the Levitical code of the
Lev. Mosaic law: "And on the eighth day the flesh
12:3 of his foreskin shall be circumcised."

In view of all this we note with some interest in the story of the conquest of Palestine that Joshua was commanded, "Make flint knives
Josh. and circumcise the people of Israel again the
5:2 second time." Later it is explained that it was their children who needed to be circumcised.

Scholars explain here that this was a kind of asseveration of the significance of the original law in this regard. Others suggest that there may have been some converts to the group by this time. But they would most likely have been circumcised Semites too. Anyway it was (and is) obligatory that converts to Judaism, if they had not already been circumcised, had to have the operation performed at whatever age.

One group of people in the early days of the Old Testament were distinguished by the fact that they did not practice circumcision. These were the Philistines, a people of Aegean origin, who settled on the coast of Palestine and began to move inland shortly after the Hebrew tribes had occupied the west bank of the Jordan. It was inevitable that the two groups would clash. Sometimes these people were referred to with the adjective "uncircumcised" before their name; and sometimes by the epithet alone. Samson's parents said to him,
Judg. "Is there not a woman among the daughters of
14:3 your kinsmen, or among all our people, that you
must go to take a wife from the uncircumcised
Philistines?" He did take a Philistine wife, but
Judg. later prayed to God that when he died he would
15:18 not "fall into the hands of the uncircumcised."
When Jonathan was fighting his nation's wars
and was about to take the offensive, he said to
his armor bearer, "Come, let us go over to the
I Sam. garrison of these uncircumcised. . . ." And
14:6 so it goes through many pages of the Old
Testament.

One of the most interesting references to circumcision has to do with the marriage of David to King Saul's daughter Michal. The *I Sam. 18:25* king desired nothing less as a bride-price for his daughter than one hundred Philistine foreskins! There was only one way to get them, and the ambitious David complied.

The next most interesting reference—purely from the standpoint of curiosity—is from one of the books of the Maccabees in the Apocrypha, a work that the Jewish historians themselves consider completely authentic. This passage refers to a period of intense religious syncretism when many young Jews wanted to conceal from others one of the essential marks of their Judaism. During the Hellenistic period after Alexander the Great, everyone in the world, it seemed, wanted to be as Greek as possible. This meant going to the gymnasium regularly and participating in the games—in which the contestants traditionally wore *I Macc. 1:14* absolutely nothing. We read that at this time many Jews "removed the marks of circumcision" so as to appear as Gentiles. How one could do this is not explained; but it must have been something familiar to the ancient world. It is mentioned again by the Apostle Paul who *I Cor. 7:18* states in one place that it was not necessary "to remove the marks of circumcision."

Jesus Christ himself never voiced any con- *Luke 2:21* cern about circumcision, although he had submitted to the rite, being an infant at the time and having no say in the matter.

Timothy, a companion of Paul, had not at first been circumcised, although he had had a Jewish mother. But his father was Greek and Greeks did not circumcise. Although Paul himself had just recently convinced the elders at Jerusalem that converts to the new faith needed not submit to the operation of circumcision,
Acts he required it of Timothy—in fact, he performed
16:3 the rite himself—in order to satisfy certain elements among the Jewish-Christians (yes, that's what many of them were), who might not exactly have considered Timothy to have been a Gentile convert because of his Jewish mother.
Col. Thereafter, however, Paul began to preach that
3:11 circumcision and non-circumcision were both the same in Christ. One might say that, from that point on, Christianity was launched as a new religion entirely apart from Judaism.

17

NAKEDNESS

NAKEDNESS in the Bible is associated with
shame—and with sex. Before they fell from
Gen. grace Adam and Eve "were both naked, and
2:25 were not ashamed." But after their sin, or sex,
3:7 or both, "they knew that they were naked;
and they sewed fig leaves together and made themselves aprons." Forever after this the people of the Bible were heavily clothed, as the bedouin is to this day. To a certain extent this was to protect the skin from the sun, but it was also associated with shame.

To see the nakedness of another is somehow to disarm him, to have him at your disposal so to speak, to have shared something that is too intimate and personal to take casually. One of the early stories of Genesis reveals the results of seeing another's nakedness in a most startling way. It is the story of Noah's son Ham, or Canaan, seeing his father's nakedness, after which he experienced acute disgrace. Noah, it seems, was the first to plant a vineyard. He was also the first to make wine and to get drunk. When this happened, we are told, he lay uncovered in his tent. His son Ham—or grandson Canaan—saw his nakedness and told the other two sons outside. Next we read:

> Then Shem and Japheth took a garment, laid it upon both their shoulders, and walked backward and covered the nakedness of their
> *Gen. 9:23–25* father; their faces were turned away, and they did not see their father's nakedness. When Noah awoke from his wine and knew what his youngest son had done to him, he said,
>
> "Cursed be Canaan;
> a slave of slaves shall he be to his brothers."

This has nothing to do with any kind of justification for black slavery as was once claimed by some racists. The Canaanites were not black anyway. The passage may be an attempt to provide some justification for the Israelites' later enslavement of the remaining Canaanites, who became "hewers of wood and bearers of water." But that is not the main point of the story, which is that the Israelites were trying to say that the Canaanites were guilty of gross sexual debauchery—especially homosexuality—which, of course, they were. And it is symbolized by seeing or uncovering the father's nakedness.

Lev. 20:11 We are told that the man "who lies with his father's wife has uncovered his father's nakedness" (as well as his stepmother's). And if one

does no more than see the nakedness of his
Lev. sister, even if only a half-sister, "it is a shameful
20:17 thing." There are numerous other examples.
But note that the shame here really has to do
with the guilt of consanguinity. There is certainly
no indication that sexual relations between
husband and wife are shameful. Nevertheless,
even between married persons, there is a
tremendous shyness in regard to nudity. When
Jacob married the first daughter of Laban and
Gen. took her to his tent for the night, he did not
29:25 know which sister he had married until the
next day.

The first king of Israel on one occasion
engaged in a rather furious bout of prophecy,
in the midst of which he stripped off his clothes
I Sam. and then fell down and lay naked all one day
19:24 and night. But the Bible elsewhere indicates
that King Saul was guilty of all kinds of erratic
behavior, bordering even on mental illness.
Actually in this case he was indulging in
something called religious ecstasy. With this
excuse one could get away with almost anything. David used this rationale when he
danced so furiously before the Ark of the
LORD as it was being brought into Jerusalem.
He was clad only in a linen ephod (apron)
and must have been quite carried away, for his
II Sam. wife Michal later accused him of uncovering
6:20 himself "as one of the vulgar fellows shamelessly
uncovers himself!" In his answer to her, David
tried to justify his behavior, contending that it
was warranted by the occasion. Her words,

however, reveal a more typical Old Testament attitude than his.

The prophet Isaiah walked "naked and
Isa. barefoot for three years," so he says, in order to
20:3 dramatize a prophecy. Of course the prophets
were overly dramatic about everything. Isaiah
was trying to warn the people how they would
be carried away into exile—stripped bare.
Such was the custom for conquered peoples;
to be stripped and carried away naked was a
Rev. way their conquerors had of shaming them.
3:18 Nakedness is associated with shame all the way
16:15 to the book of Revelation.

Job, when he had lost everything, said quite
Job. shamelessly, "Naked I came from my mother's
1:21 womb, and naked shall I return. . . ." At
last in death there is no shame.

18

APHRODISIACS AND INDUCERS OF FERTILITY

THERE IS NO scientific proof that plants, fruits, spices, or any foods produce sexual desire, but the ancients believed that som of them did, especially certain spices mixed with wine. In the Song of Solomon the bride—or whoever the girl is—delivers the following speech:

O that you were like a brother to me,
 that nursed at my mother's breast!
If I met you outside, I would kiss you,
 and none would despise me.
I would lead you and bring you
 into the house of my mother,
 and into the chamber of her that conceived me.
I would give you spiced wine to drink,
 the juice of my pomegranates.
O that his left hand were under my head,
 and that his right hand embraced me!

Song 8:1–3

Since the last two lines describe one of the basic positions for sexual intercourse, the

Song spiced wine is obviously offered as a sexual
2:5 inducement. Various fruits (apples, raisins, and
4:13–14 pomegranates) and spices (saffron and cinnamon) are mentioned in the same book. Of
course none of them is really an aphrodisiac;
but they do help to make a pleasant setting for
love-making. This is especially true of some of
the olfactory spices (spikenard and frankin-
cense) and plants (mandrakes and pomegranates), which might create a kind of psychedelic
atmosphere for love.

Wine of course has been used both in and
out of Holy Writ as a pre-course to love. Since
the days of the judges the Israelites were well
Judg. aware that it was the fruit of the vine that
9:13 "cheers gods and men." In fact, long, long
before this we had the story of Lot and his
daughters who said to each other, "Come, let
Gen. us make our father drink wine, and we will lie
19:32 with him, that we may preserve offspring
Esth. through our father." In the book of Esther we
1:10–12 read that "when the heart of the king was merry
with wine" he sent for his queen. Queen Vashti's
refusal to appear not only led to her deposition
but to the selection of Esther, the new queen.
In the apocryphal book of Judith we see how
the commander Holofernes wanted to get
Judith Judith drunk simply for the purpose of
12:16–20 seducing her. Instead he became drunk himself,
passed out, and literally lost his head. Examples
are numerous.

Among the foods of Egypt that the Israelites,
while wandering in the wilderness, claimed to

Num. miss most were meat and fish, as well as "the
11:5 cucumbers, the melons, the leeks, the onions, and the garlic." According to one doctor and rabbinical scholar, what the Israelites were really wailing about in this instance was the loss of the aphrodisiacal powers believed to be contained in these foods, or in some of them anyway.* Fish, or seafood, for centuries has been thought to be an aphrodisiac, for Aphrodite or Love in ancient Mediterranean thought was believed to have arisen from the sea. Vegetables that were phallic shaped were also believed to possess this quality, as well as certain bulbous vegetables, for reasons unknown.

One of the plants mentioned in the Song of
Song Solomon is mandrakes. This flower, or its root,
7:13 was believed to be an inducer of fertility, so much so that the childless Rachel pleads for them in the following story from Genesis:

> In the days of wheat harvest Reuben went and found mandrakes in the field, and brought them to his mother Leah. Then Rachel said to Leah, "Give me, I pray, some of your son's mandrakes." But she said to her, "Is it a small matter that you have taken away my husband? Would you take away my son's mandrakes also?" Rachel said, "Then he may lie with you tonight for your son's mandrakes." When Jacob came

*C. J. Brim, *Medicine in the Bible* (New York: Froben Press, 1936), p. 357.

> *Gen.* from the field in the evening, Leah went out
> *30:14–24* to meet him, and said, "You must come in to
> me; for I have hired you with my son's mandrakes." So he lay with her that night. . . . Then God remembered Rachel, and God hearkened to her and opened her womb. She conceived and bore a son, and said, "God has taken away my reproach"; and she called his name Joseph.

The mandrake is a Mediterranean herb of the night-shade family, which, our sources tell us, was "formerly used especially to promote conception."*

Far more common were the fertility symbols. We read that in the days of Rehoboam, the son of Solomon, the people of Judah "built for themselves high places, and pillars, and
I Kgs. Asherim on every high hill and under every
14:23 green tree." The "pillars" were phallic-shaped
columns and the Asherim upright poles representing the mother goddess, both of which were believed to be inducers of fertility. Note that the Old Testament is speaking disparagingly. Their use must have been widespread for them to merit so much condemnation.

Some have gone so far as to suggest that even
Gen. the Tower of Babel was a phallic symbol. If
11:1–9 so, this was lost on the Old Testament, in which
the Tower was condemned but for other reasons. If one is really looking for sexual

* *Webster's*, 1971.

symbolism in a culture, he can probably find it anyplace. But when the Bible's authors, especially in the Old Testament, wanted to write about sexual imagery, both male and female, they usually did so in more concrete terms. Let us turn now to a discussion of that subject.

19

THE SEXUAL ORGANS*

THE BIBLE has a proper respect for the sexual organs, both male and female. The male organ mentioned most often is of course the penis, while the female organ referred to most often is the womb. Breasts too are a recurring sexual theme, and there are others, as we shall see.

The word penis itself is not used but there are a variety of euphemisms. Men themselves are referred to exactly half a dozen times in the *King James Version* by the picturesque phrase,
I Sam. 25:22 "any that pisseth against the wall."† The *Revised Standard Version* has simply the word "male" in place of that awkward phrase. "Loins" is a common expression for all of the genitalia, both male and female, and for the nearby intestinal area as well, but in the majority of cases in which it is used it pertains to men. It is found as many as seventy times in the *King James Version*. The *Revised Standard Version*

*This chapter also treats a few other parts of the body that have to do with sexual attraction, as well as the sexual organs per se.

†Other references are I Sam. 25: 34; I Kgs. 14:10, 16:11, 21:21; and II Kgs. 9:8.

includes more precise expressions, such as "their vessels" and "things." Sometimes, as mentioned previously, the text will say "feet" when it is really referring to the genitalia.

In the little book of Ruth there is a very unusual reference in which the word "feet" is clearly a euphemism for the male genitals. The young widow Ruth, acting on instructions from an older woman, went to the threshing floor where her future husband was sleeping after
Ruth having drunk heavily. There, in the middle of
3:7 of the night, she "uncovered his feet, and lay down." She was obviously making a marriage proposal to an older man who never dreamed that she would be interested in him. How do we know that it is a marriage proposal and not just a proposition? Because if Boaz had not received permission the next day from Ruth's nearest of kin to marry her, and if her escapade with him were later discovered through her pregnancy, the poor girl would have been stoned as an adulteress. For she still belonged to her dead husband, so to speak, until given in marriage to another.

We learn in the early histories that before going into battle, or even when on any kind of military expedition, the soldiers were supposed to have "kept themselves from women." David said on one occasion to the priest who questioned him about his companions: "Of a truth women have been kept
I Sam. from us as always when I go on an expedition;
21:5 the vessels of the young men are holy, even

when it is a common journey; how much more today will their vessels be holy?"

Another custom among the men, which is mentioned only in connection with the very earliest period of the Old Testament, was their formula for swearing oaths by having one of them—that is, the one who was making the vow—first put forth his hand and touch the sexual organ, or organs, of the other man as he repeated the words required of him. We read
Gen. that Abraham addressed his servant: "Put
24:2–3 your hand under my thigh, and I will make you
swear by the LORD, the God of heaven and of
the earth. . . . " A few verses further down we
24:9 read: "So the servant put his hand under the
thigh of Abraham his master, and swore to him concerning the matter." Now the most important organs "under the thigh" that one could touch in keeping with the solemnity of the occasion would be either the penis or the testicles (or both). Then the other man most likely responded by returning the same gesture, and woe be unto him who broke such an oath! Loss of one or more of the organs involved was the probable penalty. The only other reference that we have to this early custom proves that it was not something that could be required only of servants. Jacob, when he was nearing death, called his son Joseph to him and said, "If now
Gen. I have found favor in your sight, put your hand
47:29 under my thigh, and promise to deal loyally
and truly with me."

The most unusual reference to the principal

male sexual organ is in the advice given to
Rehoboam, son of Solomon, when the elders
of Israel come to him after his father's death to
ask that their burdens be made lighter. His
advisors counseled him to say to them, "My
I Kgs. little finger is thicker than my father's loins."
12:10 It is a way of saying "you will feel my little
finger heavier upon you than you would my
father's penis." It is a shocking speech, and as
a result of it the Kingdom of Israel was literally
split into two parts.

In one of the prophetical books, the sexual
Ezek. organs of Egyptian men are compared to those
23:20 of asses. This could mean that they were large
but quite hideous.

A woman should remember always to treat
a man's sexual organs with proper respect,
according to the Bible. One of the most interesting of all the Deuteronomic laws is that
known as the Law of the Immodest Woman. It
says that if two men are fighting and the wife of
one of them decides to come to the aid of her
Deut. husband, she is under no circumstances to take
25:11–12 hold of his opponent's "private parts." If she
does so, the guilty hand is to be chopped off!
Furthermore the community is admonished to
have no pity on such an immodest woman.

Speaking of the congregation or Old Testament church, the law says, "He whose testicles
Deut. are crushed or whose male member is cut off
23:1 shall not enter the assembly of the LORD."
The very next verse after this one says that no
"bastards" are to enter. This law, if enforced,

Deut. would keep a lot of people out of church.
23:2 Also, one who has "crushed testicles" is ineligible for the priesthood. The only reason given
Lev. for this is that one who has such a "blemish"
21:17–21 should not "offer the bread of his God."

One of the prophets predicted that the king
Isa. of Assyria would shave with a razor "the head
7:20 and the hair of the feet" of the Israelites as he
carried them into exile, which in fact did
happen. "Feet" refers to the male organs and
"hair" here is pubic hair. The pubic genital hair
of the female, according to the Hebrew
Ezek. lexicon, is specifically referred to once in the
16:7 Bible, and it is in the context—of all things
—of a *sermon* by one of the major prophets!

As for the female sexual organs, the breasts are the all-important things. These parts of the female anatomy seem to be referred to from beginning to end of the little Song of Solomon, but nowhere more erotically than here:

How fair and pleasant you are,
O loved one, delectable maiden!
You are stately as a palm tree,
and your breasts are like its clusters.
I say I will climb the palm tree
and lay hold of its branches.
Song Oh, may your breasts be like clusters of
7:6–9 the vine,
and the scent of your breath like apples,
and your kisses like the best wine
that goes down smoothly,
gliding over lips and teeth.

Song Earlier he had said that her two breasts were
4:5 like "two fawns, twins of a gazelle."
7:3 Near the end of the same book the bridegroom or male singer seems very worried about his little sister "because she has no breasts." "What shall we do with our sister on the day when she is spoken for?" Does this mean that
Song she would be passed up as a prospective bride?
8:8–10 So it seems. He says that if she is like a wall (flat-chested), then we must add silver embellishments; if she is like a door, we must add cedar paneling! At this point his own girl friend reminds him that she herself is like a wall, but one with twin towers (her breasts).

As for the other parts of the female anatomy, lovely eyes were of utmost importance. Perhaps in many cases this was the only part of the girl's face that the prospective bridegroom saw. We are told that Jacob preferred Rachel over
Gen. Leah, but of their appearance only that "Leah's
29:17 eyes were weak, but Rachel was beautiful and lovely." Also a big nose was a good thing. The
Song Song of Solomon says of the bride, "Your
7:4 nose is like a tower of Lebanon, overlooking Damascus." Such a nose would give a nice profile to a face that was veiled. Other than that we can offer no explanation.

In the same stanza the lover sings:

Your rounded thighs are like jewels,
the work of a master hand.
Song Your navel is a rounded bowl
7:1–2 that never lacks wine.

The last two lines above indicate that oral eroticism was not unknown. The next two lines we quote are proof of it:

Song 4:11

> Your lips distill nectar, my bride;
> honey and milk are under your tongue.

And in the same verse, there is a reference to garment sniffing:

> the scent of your garments is like
> the scent of Lebanon.

This erotic book also has the lover say of his beloved, not once but on two occasions:

Song 4:1 6:5

> Your hair is like a flock of goats,
> moving down the slopes of Gilead.

We do not know whether he is enthralled with its fleecy appearance or its musty smell. Considering that the Old Testament is in general very earthy in its approach, the latter is most likely.

"Womb" (or "belly") is mentioned in the entire Bible almost seventy times, usually in connection with conception and child-bearing. But it is obviously a kind of all-inclusive term, for the actual female genitals (clitoris and vagina) are not mentioned specifically.

The "barren womb," however, is referred to in one of the most vivid pieces of hyperbole in the Bible:

Three things are never satisfied;
  four never say "Enough";
Prov. 30:15–16 Sheol, the barren womb,
  the earth ever thirsty for water,
  and the fire which never says, "Enough."

The barren womb is willing to keep trying forever until a child is conceived.

But the very idea of "barrenness" is in the Bible a special topic to which we should devote at least a few pages at this time.

20

BARRENNESS AND FERTILITY

THESE TOPICS should quite logically be discussed together, for one was the exact opposite of the other. Barrenness was a curse, fertility a blessing. Or it could be stated: children were a blessing for a married couple, the lack of them was a curse.

Sons were especially desirable, for they were their parents' social security in their old age and their memorial after death. The idea goes back to the prehistory of the Old Testament. The bedouin, who was constantly on the move, could not erect any kind of memorial for himself, not even a tombstone. Sons would have to serve in this capacity. They were tremendously important. The psalmist sings:

Lo, sons are a heritage from the LORD,
 the fruit of the womb a reward.
Like arrows in the hand of a warrior
 are the sons of one's youth. *Ps. 127:3–5*
Happy is the man who has
 his quiver full of them!

He shall not be put to shame
when he speaks with his enemies in
the gate.

Job, both before and after his trials and
Job tribulations, was considered almost the perfect
1:2 man. He had seven sons and three daughters,
42:13 twice as many boys, plus one, as girls—the
ideal arrangement.

Grandchildren, presumably even coming from one's daughter, were a good thing. A good
Ps. wish to extend to someone was: "May you see
128:6 your children's children!"

The people of Biblical times did not know about the problem of sterility in certain men: if a married man had not fathered a child before coming to old age, he too was thought to be under some kind of a curse from God.* But the word "barren" was used only of women. And barrenness—if she was subject to it—was the biggest problem of her life.

A man's wife, the psalmist says, should be
Ps. like a "fruitful vine." This meant that the
128:3 couple had been blessed by God. There are so many illustrations to support this point of view that we could not list them all without greatly enlarging this chapter. But there is no need to quote all of the references. Even the casual reader of the Bible very quickly senses the tremendous importance of children. Our task in this book is not primarily to call

*They knew, of course, about the possibility of impotence in older men, as for example in II Kings 4: 14.

attention to the obvious, but rather to point out to readers what they might otherwise miss. One such thing is the absolute awfulness of the curse of barrenness in women.

The first in the Bible to be afflicted with this curse was Sarah, the wife of Abraham. However, she did not have to bemoan her barren-
Gen. ness too much, for her husband did it for her.
15:2 Or perhaps he was lamenting for himself.
Sarah decided that she would have a child of sorts anyway, by giving her maid Hagar to Abraham, "that I shall obtain children by her." Abraham obliged, but after the servant
Gen. had conceived, she looked upon her mistress
16:1–6 with contempt. Therefore the maid and her
Gen. child Ishmael were eventually driven out of the
18:1–15 household. Later Sarah conceived, after the
21:1–7 visitation of angels.

Rebekah, the wife of Isaac, was at first
Gen. barren but because of her husband's prayers
25:21 she later conceived and bore him twin sons,
Esau and Jacob. In cases of twin sons, the one who "comes out" first had priority according to the Law of Primogeniture, or the "law of
Deut. the firstborn." It was the same as if he were
21:17 born a year or so before the other; he was the
firstborn, and the firstborn inherited a double share of the father's property or possessions. (Girls did not count in this arrangement.)
Gen. Jacob, who was born only a short time after
27 Esau, refused to accept second place and
"bought" or "tricked" his way into first position.

Rachel, favorite wife of Jacob, was also barren at first. Whereas her sister Leah, also married to Jacob, was fertile, for "when the LORD saw that Leah was hated, he opened
Gen. 29:31 her womb." The Bible presents this as a kind of compensation for the fact that she did not have her husband's love. At least she had children. Many a wife has had to learn to be content with as little or less. Leah learned to live with the situation somehow. But Rachel, even with her husband's love, was not content without children. She said to Jacob, "Give me
Gen. 30:1–2 children, or I shall die!" Jacob snapped back, "Am I in the place of God, who has withheld from you the fruit of the womb?" Rachel was
Gen. 30:14–24 eventually granted fertility, with the help of mandrakes, as we have seen in chapter eighteen.

The next case of a barren woman in the Old Testament was the mother of Samson. She was barren, that is, until "an angel of the LORD" appeared to her and announced that she would
Judg. 13:2–5 have a son. But there was a stipulation. The son was to be a Nazirite—that is, one who should not cut his hair or drink wine—throughout his lifetime. Some people think of Nazirites as constituting a religious order. They did not. They were simply individuals who were under a vow for a certain length of time. There were no religious orders in the Bible at all.

No one in the Bible bemoans her barrenness more than Hannah, the mother of Samuel. Perhaps she was goaded on because she was chided by her husband's other wife, who was fertile. Hannah not only wept and refused to eat, but on periodic visits to the old shrine at *I Sam. 1–2* Shiloh she wept loudly in the sanctuary and cried out that if God would grant her a son she would give him back to the Lord to serve all the days of his life. Her prayer was granted, and no sooner was the boy "weaned" than she took him to the sanctuary and left him there to be trained for religious service. (But note that, according to custom, the boy may not have been weaned until he was well past the infancy stage.) The Song of Thanksgiving that she sang at that moment was the literary model for the Magnificat or "Song of Mary," which the latter sang when she was pregnant with the *Luke 1:46–55* baby Jesus. Hannah's son grew up to become the prophet Samuel who was instrumental in founding the Israelite nation in that he selected and anointed its first two kings.

The final case of the barren woman in the Bible is Mary's cousin, Elizabeth, the mother *Luke 1:5–80* of John the Baptist. Often the curse of barrenness continued into old age, which made the eventual birth of the child seem miraculous or, at least, extremely unusual. Such was the situation of Sarah, the first example we mentioned, and it was also the case with Elizabeth, our last example. Otherwise the pattern was familiar. The husband also was old. The child to be born was to drink no wine. When it was born the mother said that God had at last taken away her "reproach." Finally, the child born of this situation grew up to be no ordinary individual but one under the very special providence of God.

But, in whatever case, fertility was from God; it was a divine gift, a blessing from God Most High. Furthermore, if one had this
Deut. 28:1–12 blessing it was thoroughgoing. It extended not only to the fruit of your body, but to the fruit of your cattle and the fruit of your ground; even to your basket and to your kneading-trough. Of course it was contingent upon your obedience and upon God's love. If you did not obey:

> Cursed shall you be in the city, and cursed shall you be in the field. Cursed shall be your basket and your kneading-trough. Cursed shall be the fruit of your body, and the fruit
> *Deut. 28:16–19* of your ground, the increase of your cattle, and the young of your flock. Cursed shall you be when you come in, and cursed shall you be when you go out.

"Cursed" here implies "barrenness"; and "Cursed shall be the fruit of your body" here means either that there will not be any fruit, or if there is any, it will all be rotten.

21

VIRGINITY

VIRGINITY, or the lack of it, was something the Old Testament did not take lightly. For a girl to be marriageable, she had to be a virgin. An "experienced" potential bride, if her secret were known, had no chance at all in the marriage market. But young girls were so protected in the ancient East that the probability of their having had any pre-marital sexual relations was almost nil.

Gen. 24:16 When Rebekah was being considered as the future wife of Isaac, this is how she was described: "The maiden was fair to look upon, a virgin, whom no man had known." In the book of Esther, when the king of Persia was searching for a new queen, his servants said to him:

Esth. 2:2–4 Let beautiful young virgins be sought out for the king. And let the king appoint officers in all the provinces of his kingdom to gather all the beautiful young virgins to the harem in Susa the capital, under custody of Hegai the king's eunuch who is in charge of the

> women; let their ointments be given them. And let the maiden who pleases the king be queen instead of Vashti.

It was not only bedouin girls and queens who had to be virginal. The prophet Isaiah, in commenting on whom the average man married, said, "a young man marries a virgin." *Isa. 62:5* Old men did, too, whenever they could. For a priest it was a requirement of the law that he do so. *Lev. 21:14*

There was even a test for ascertaining whether or not a young bride was a virgin. If the husband felt any doubt, "then the father of the young woman and her mother shall take and bring out the tokens of her virginity" and show them "to the elders of the city in the gate." If the parents of the bride were upheld in the verdict, the accusing husband was to be whipped, then was to take his bride home, not to put her away "all his days." But if he were upheld in the verdict, then the bride was to be stoned to death. *Deut. 22:13–21* All of this is discussed in the context of hypothetical or case law—that is, what to do in such and such a case. We have no way of knowing if these occurrences were common. The interesting point, however, is the clear implication that on the wedding night one had to look for the physical evidence of virginity (on the bedding or nightgown!) and hold on to it just in case an accusation might be forthcoming.

One of the laws of Moses states that there was a marriage price for virgins:

Exod. 22:16–17

> If a man seduces a virgin who is not betrothed, and lies with her, he shall give the marriage present for her, and make her his wife. If her father utterly refuses to give her to him, he shall pay money equivalent to the marriage present for virgins.

Judg. 11:37–39

Jephthah's daughter, who was sacrificed by her father in payment of a rash vow, asked for a two month reprieve "that I may go and wander on the mountains, and bewail my virginity, I and my companions." The request was granted, and at the end of the period she returned and the vow was fulfilled. The text says sadly, "She had never known a man." Her father had promised to offer up whoever was the first to come forth from the doors of his house when he returned victorious from battle. His only daughter was the victim. In spite of the peculiar circumstances of this vow, one gets the feeling that had she not been a virgin, she would have been ineligible to be the victim. It was her virginity she was offering, as well as her life.

Judg. 21:12

In one unusual story, four hundred young virgins "who had not known any man by lying with them" were rounded up to marry the surviving male members of the tribe of Benjamin. This incident was preceded by an inter-tribal war in which supposedly all of the females of the tribe of Benjamin had been killed or taken as booty of war. But the four hundred virgins were not enough. The single men of Benjamin

were then advised to go to the annual wine
Judg festival at Shiloh and "steal" brides from
21:16–24 among the maidens who came to dance at the
festival there. This story is quite similar to the
Roman myth of the Rape of the Sabine Women,
which was not so much a rape as a way of
getting marriageable young girls for the single
men of Rome.

In one of the prophetical books, Israel herself
is called a virgin, fallen, "with none to raise
her up." It is one of the most beautiful—and
at the same time pathetic—personifications
in the whole Bible:

Fallen, no more to rise,
Amos is the virgin Israel;
5:2 forsaken on her land,
with none to raise her up.

Matt. In the New Testament, the Gospels of
1:18–24 Matthew and of Luke include accounts of Jesus'
Luke virgin birth, his mother Mary having been
1:26–37 impregnated by a visitation of the Holy Ghost.
But the Gospels of Mark and of John do not
mention it, nor is it referred to elsewhere in the
Bible. Nevertheless, after the period of the
New Testament, some churches began to go so
far as to declare that Mary was "ever-virginal."
Matt. But if she was the mother of the several
13:55 brothers and sisters of Jesus who are mentioned
in the gospels, then she certainly could not
Mark have been perpetually pure. It has been sug-
6:3 gested that these "brothers" and "sisters"

were the children of Joseph by a former marriage. In any case, it is unlikely that the young wife of a normal man then or at any other time would have remained ever-virginal.

Matt. Jesus told a parable about ten virgins, five
25:1–13 wise and five foolish, using the term simply in the sense of "young girls" or "maidens." Actually they were marriageable young girls who, according to the custom, were serving as bridesmaids for a girlfriend or family member. Both ancient Hebrew and Greek had specific words for "virgin," but they were used primarily when one wanted to emphasize the sexual innocence of the girl in question. In day-to-day conversation in both languages the words for "young girl" were used, not precluding the fact that the girl was a virgin. On the contrary, it was very definitely understood that she was.

All of this relates to the hullabaloo that broke out a few years ago when the *Revised Standard Version* appeared with a new rendi-
Isa. tion of the famous prophecy from Isaiah. The
7:14 *King James* had read: "Behold a virgin shall conceive, and bear a son. . . ." The new translation said: "Behold, a young woman shall conceive and bear a son"; and the National Council of the Churches of Christ (in the U.S.A.), which had sponsored the offending version, was beset with dissension and division. Actually the Hebrew text of the passage in question does say "young woman" or "young girl." The *King James Version* had relied

upon the Greek translation of the Hebrew Bible, and the Greek had interpreted the word as "virgin." But the whole thing was and is a ridiculous argument. Virginal was what every young girl in ancient Israel—and Greece—was fully expected to be.

22

UNUSUAL LOVE STORIES AND ALLUSIONS

THE OLDEST reference to a very free-wheeling or "swinging" kind of sex is in the sixth chapter of the Bible. We read that there were Nephilim or "giants in the earth in those days." How did they come about? It happened that "the sons of God"—angels or semi-divine beings—looked around and "saw that the daughters of men were fair; and they took to wife such as they chose." These sons of God "came in to the daughters of men," and children were born to them. This accounts for a race of "mighty men of old, the men of renown," mentioned here and elsewhere in the text. It also corresponds precisely to the Age of the Heroes in ancient Greece. They too were spawned by divine fathers and human mothers. One of them was Hercules.

Gen. 6:1–4

Gen. 10:8–9

The Old Testament character most comparable to Hercules was Samson. Both of these heroes, as their first public deed, killed a lion with their bare hands. Samson was, in fact, too good not to be true. Physically he was supra-human, but one thing eluded him: the knack of understanding women, and in that respect he was definitely human. Samson married a Philistine girl, but when he went off on one of his exploits the girl's father gave her to another man. His excuse to Samson was:

> I really thought that you utterly hated her;
> *Judg. 15:2* so I gave her to your companion. Is not her younger sister fairer than she? Pray, take her instead.

But Samson did not take her. Instead he visited harlots. Finally he loved another Philistine
Judg. 16:4–30 woman whose name was Delilah. They had quite an affair, one of the most celebrated affairs of all time, if one considers the opera and films. There is no mention of their ever having been married. Unfortunately this girl was Samson's undoing, but he brought down quite a few Philistines with him.

The little book of Ruth is perhaps the most charming love story in the Bible and an exquisite piece of world literature. It contains one of the most beautiful love poems ever
Ruth 1:16–17 uttered (see chapter 24: "Love Poems of the Bible"), which, as it happened, was delivered by a girl to—of all people—her mother-in-law!* The real romance of the book, as already

*Louise Pettibone Smith, writing in the *Interpreter's Bible*, has compared the friendship of Ruth and Naomi to that of David and Jonathan—but only in the sense that the two women were true "friends." II (1953), 813.

noted, was between Ruth and an older man, Boaz. It begins literally "once upon a time" and ends practically by saying "they lived happily ever after." For a short story, the book has tremendous dramatic qualities. In each scene there are two characters principally on stage, and one of them moves off, leaving the other; or they both move off and leave a third. It ends like this:

Ruth 4:13–17

> So Boaz took Ruth and she became his wife; and he went in to her, and the LORD gave her conception, and she bore a son. . . . They named him Obed he was the father of Jesse, the father of David.

We have already mentioned David and Jonathan, and David and Bathsheba. The apparent bisexuality of the Old Testament's greatest hero is presented without so much as the batting of an eye—or eyelash.

I Kgs. 10:1–13

One of the most famous stories of love in the Bible is more tradition than fact. This is the alleged physical union that took place between David's son Solomon and the Queen of Sheba. To this day the Ethiopian royal house traces its lineage to this most celebrated of all foreign affairs, and the present monarch of Ethiopia has among his royal titles, "Lion of Judah." Actually the Old Testament text does not say that they slept together. What it does say is that the queen paid the king a royal visit, arriving with enough luggage to spend the year if she liked. After seeing what Solomon had to offer, she said that "the half was not told me." Then we are told: "And King Solomon gave to the queen of Sheba all that she desired, whatever she asked. . . . "

One of several books of the Old Testament (and of the Apocrypha) attributed to King Solomon is Ecclesiastes, probably because it describes a king who had had everything and done everything. Or so its introduction
says. Later it adds that for everything there is
Eccl. a season, even "a time for love." It also says,
3:1–8 "Again, if two lie together they are warm;
4:11 but how can one be warm alone?"

Another work attributed to Solomon is the Proverbs. Women, and how men are to feel about them, pro and con, is one of the major
motifs of the book. On the one hand they are
Prov. honored, praised, and respected—primarily
31:10–31 as wives of course—but on the other hand,
the prudent young man is warned against them, especially against the kind that, for want of a better term, might be called the "loose woman." Let us consider one of the author's examples as described in a classic passage. In spite of her clothes (or the way she is dressed for this occasion), the woman in question here is no harlot. She is a dutifully religious and married woman. However, she does not let either of these factors stand in her way. The following is how the author of the book of Proverbs describes the scene:

For at the window of my house
  I have looked out through my lattice,
and I have seen among the simple,
  I have perceived among the youths,
  a young man without sense,
passing along the street near her corner,
  taking the road to her house
in the twilight, in the evening,
  at the time of night and darkness.

Prov. 7:6–23

And lo, a woman meets him,
  dressed as a harlot, wily of heart.
She is loud and wayward,
  her feet do not stay at home;
now in the street, now in the market,
  and at every corner she lies in wait.
She seizes him and kisses him,
  and with impudent face she says to him:
"I had to offer sacrifices,
  and today I have paid my vows;
so now I have come out to meet you,
  to seek you eagerly, and I have found you.
I have decked my couch with coverings,
  colored spreads of Egyptian linen;
I have perfumed my bed with myrrh,
  aloes and cinnamon.
Come, let us take our fill of love till morning;
  let us delight ourselves with love.
For my husband is not at home;
  he has gone on a long journey;
he took a bag of money with him;
  at full moon he will come home."

With much seductive speech she persuades
 him;
 with her smooth talk she compels him.
All at once he follows her,
 as an ox goes to the slaughter,
or as a stag is caught fast
 till an arrow pierces its entrails;
as a bird rushes into a snare;
 he does not know that it will cost him his
 life.

Actually this account need not represent a historical occurrence but a kind of summation of the real life observations of the author. It is advice given by the wise writer—male—to his readers—obviously other males. The seductress here is simply symbolic of folly, which the reader is admonished to avoid.

The one book in the Bible that is completely devoted to love—that is, physical love—is the little work called the Song of Solomon. In support of this position we submit the following passage:

Song 2:6 8:3

O that his left hand were under my head,
 and that his right hand embraced me.

This refers, as noted previously, to one of the basic positions of sexual intercourse and is quoted at the beginning and at the end of the book. And so it goes throughout.

There have been many theories as to the meaning of this work. Originally it had to be

love poetry, probably sung at weddings of Palestinian peasants, for there are parts of it to be said or sung by the bride, the groom, and the chorus. Thus the groom is Solomon and the bride is the Shulammite (or Shunammite). The Shunammite in Israelite history
I Kgs. 1:3–4 was the sexy little creature who was fetched to keep King David's bed warm in his extreme old age. It must have been his "extreme old age" because the text says that "the king knew her not." King Solomon logically inherited his father's concubines along with his father's other property—and that is just what she was—and possibly she became his favorite. Hence the association here. But a concubine could never become queen, except perhaps for a day—or a night.

Paul of Tarsus, who generally had a rather puritanical attitude toward sex, ironically wrote one of the most beautiful hymns to love ever composed. "If I speak in the tongues of men and
I Cor. 13:1–13 of angels, but have not love, I am a noisy gong or a clanging cymbal. . . . So faith, hope, love abide, these three; but the greatest of these is love." The hymn throughout sounds as if it could be speaking of physical as well as spiritual love, about which Paul was really concerned. The hymn sounds a note that the Bible as a whole would confirm, and that is that love—if it is real love—is both spiritual and
I John 4:16 physical. For "God is love, and he who abides in love abides in God, and God abides in him."

23
JESUS CHRIST AND SEX

WE HAVE COVERED enough ground by this time, hopefully, to have learned that the Bible is hardly prudish on the subject of sex. It told it as it was, so to speak, centuries before it was fashionable to do so. It knew and it depicted life as it was lived, while at the same
I Cor. time trying, as Paul said, to point out "a more
12:31 excellent way."

As each topic was covered we have tried to present the material that the Bible itself contains on the subject, in a more or less logical or chronological order. That being the case, the view of Jesus Christ on this or that subject has been presented along with the rest. But it was felt that the entire subject would be lacking if we were to avoid the one topic which, for the most part throughout history, Christians seldom if ever mention—and that is, Jesus Christ and sex. The Christian position—if there has been one at all—has been basically that the Master was above such matters. This position is derived of course from the stance of Christian faith. To a very great extent these conclusions are justified, but for a different reason. The reason is clearly the lack of evidence. What we have are the Gospels of Matthew, Mark, Luke, and John, these four and no more. But from any scholarly standpoint these writings are testimonials of faith, not biographies in our sense of that word. Nevertheless they do record—some forty to seventy-five years after his crucifixion—what the early Christians believed about Jesus. Hence we will make a few comments on the basis of what they contain.

First of all, they say nothing about his appearance but, nevertheless, indicate that people were tremendously drawn to him. He has been depicted in art, carved, cast, and painted, more than any other subject who has ever lived. He has generally been portrayed as a rather attractive and moving figure, somewhat fragile but none the less a man. He died when he was at the peak of his manhood, at about thirty-three.

He was single. If he ever considered marriage for himself the Bible does not mention it. He had, however, an extremely high regard for the institution—for others, that is—for the family, and, for his day, an unusually high regard for women. He supported the earliest Old Testament view of marriage as presented in the second chapter of Genesis, as a physical union between one man and one woman who then became "one flesh." This grew out of the general ancient Semitic idea

of the oneness of the family. But he added to it these words that are not found in the Old
Matt. 19:6 Testament: "What therefore God has joined together, let no man put asunder."

On the one hand this attitude in defense of the permanence of marriage may seem to be a rather narrow position. On the other hand it can be regarded simply as a very strong defense of the institution of marriage and the family. It may be that Jesus was trying to get across the idea that the relationship that should exist between a man and a woman is analogous to the kind of love that God has for the human family, and therefore it must be permanent. But there may have been something more. His position may very conceivably be construed as part of his high regard for women. His society afforded numerous examples of women who were set aside for more lovely rivals, and unless their own (fathers') families were sufficiently powerful there was nothing they could do about it. Nowhere do we find that Jesus downgrades the female, as was generally the accepted practice in the ancient Mediterranean and Eastern worlds.

The actual presence of women in the text is much more prominent in Luke than in any other gospel. Early in the record we read about Jesus' most intimate group as follows:

> And the twelve [disciples] were with him, and also some women who had been healed

> of evil spirits and infirmities: Mary called Magdalene, from whom seven demons
> *Luke 8:1–3* had gone out, and Joanna, the wife of Chuza, Herod's steward, and Susanna, and many others, who provided for them out of their means.

Of course one might argue that he liked them because they "provided" for him. But this was only in some cases, and it could be shown that he was equally provided for by male benefactors.

Mary, from a village called Magdala, has for ages been linked with prostitution in church tradition and in the public mind. There is *Luke 7:37* no conclusive evidence for this, although admittedly there is enough circumstantial evidence to put her under considerable suspicion. But for sinners and harlots to be converted to a new faith is nothing new. This is what we would expect. What is more startling is the suggestion that has been made that the relationship was more than a spiritual attraction of Jesus to the Magdalene and especially of the Magdalene to him. The idea was rather boldly presented by Nikos Kazantzakis (of *Zorba* fame) in one of his best but lesser known works, *The Last Temptation of Christ.** The two of them go about mooning over each other halfway through the book. She was willing, but he resisted. In fact, as Kazantzakis

*Translated from the Greek by P. A. Bien. (Simon and Schuster, 1960).

presents it, his rejection of her was what really had turned her to prostitution in the first place. Essentially the theme here is one that is a favorite with Kazantzakis: the tension that exists between flesh and spirit.

More recently the Jesus-Magdalene liaison has been presented to us as considerably more than a leitmotif in the popular musical, *Jesus Christ Superstar.* In spite of the criticisms of this play—people just did not expect to see it staged—the theme is rather tastefully treated for so delicate a subject. She wants to but doesn't try, and she would be frigid—unusual for her—if *he* were to try, which he doesn't. That seems to be it.

Now just what is the textual justification for this? Very little, if any. Of course Mary might have been attached to him for his curing her of demonic (neurotic) addiction, for accepting her as a human being, and because he was, as for ages sermons on the subject have said, like no one she had ever known before. She was accustomed to being used by men, as a sexual object. Here was someone who treated her like a person. Naturally there would be an attachment. But it would not have to have been an attachment of a sexual nature. It is easy to jump to conclusions, but conclusions that are not based upon evidence lead to fantasy, not truth.

It has even been suggested in a recent work by William E. Phipps that Jesus was actually betrothed and married in his early manhood, as were most young people of his day.* If this was so, the gospel writers do not mention it. They are silent about a lot of other things, however; for example, what was Jesus doing the thirty years before he began his ministry? One of the chief problems with this theory of the married Jesus is: where was his wife during the years of his actual (itinerant) ministry? The author of this ingenious thesis suggests a number of things: she could have died by that time; she could have stayed home in Galilee to care for the family; she could have left Jesus and gone astray, like Mary Magdalene, becoming a prostitute herself (or perhaps she was Mary Magdalene); she could have been unable to accompany him because of frail health; or, she left him because she no longer cared to be associated with him for various reasons. Such conjecture could go on ad infinitum; and, although it is a most interesting and intriguing speculation, there is no proof of any of it. Until there is, it must remain just that: an interesting speculation, indeed.

It has also been suggested that Jesus preferred men to women.† Manuals on the history of homosexuality do not overlook the oppor-

*William E. Phipps, *Was Jesus Married*? (Harper & Row, 1970), especially pp. 66–70.

†Canon Hugh Montefiore, an Anglican theologian, at an Oxford conference presented conclusions to the effect that Jesus may have had homosexual tendencies, *Newsweek*, Aug. 7, 1967, p. 83, and the *Times* (London), Aug. 7, 1967, p. 2. Books of the past that have mentioned the subject for the most part have been of the *sub rosa* variety, the authors using pseudonyms rather than their own names.

tunity to list famous world figures who were given to this proclivity, among them Socrates, Plato, Alexander the Great, Leonardo da Vinci, Michelangelo, and so on. Some are bold enough to add Jesus to the list. Any way you look at it, it is an impressive company. But as for any evidence of homosexuality in his case, what is there?

First of all, there was the rather close relation-
Matt. ship with his mother, which is often taken to be
12:46–50 an indication of at least a tendency toward
Mark homosexuality. Three times in the course of
3:31–35 the gospels we are told that she came after
Luke him, no doubt in an effort to get him to come
8:19–21 home. In any mother and grown son relationship, this is a tell-tale sign, especially when the man is over thirty. This could also explain why she, a peasant woman, journeyed down from Galilee to Jerusalem and to her consternation ended up there at the time of the crucifixion. Secondly, for a Palestinian man still to be single at his age would raise some questions as to why. But both these factors may be purely coincidental.

John More prominent among the "evidence"
13:23 submitted are the three references in John's
19:26 Gospel to "the disciple whom Jesus loved."*
21:7 At the Last Supper, with all the disciples present, he alone "was lying close to the breast of Jesus." At the foot of the cross he is the only disciple mentioned who was "standing near," and hence to him was commended the care of

*See also John 11: 5 and 36.

Jesus' mother. Later in Galilee, after the resurrection, when the disciples had returned to fishing and the resurrected Christ appeared to call them back to discipleship, this still unnamed disciple was the first to recognize Jesus. He said to Peter, "It is the Lord," and they all rushed to shore. The name of the beloved disciple is never given, but most say that the writer of the gospel intends it to be John the Apostle; others say it was Lazarus. What are we to make of it?

In the first place, warm friendships between two men were and are accepted as customary in the Middle East. Because such friendships are commonplace, they are not suspected of being homosexual. At ancient Semitic—and at modern Arabic—banquets it is not considered unusual for one man to lean on the arms or shoulders of another. And it was customary for men who were close friends to kiss on the lips if they wished when greeting or
Rom. taking leave of each other. (This is why Paul
16:16 tells the early Christians to greet one another
I Cor. with a "holy kiss"—rather than the usual
16:20 kind.) But on the positive side of the contention that Jesus might have preferred men, if any single man today selected a group of twelve close disciples, all male, and traveled around a Western country with them, allowing one of them to lean on his chest at dinner, there would be little doubt as to what people would think!

The concept of the Twelve also merits some consideration. The idea of Christ and the

Twelve Apostles as constituting a basic order of the church is Christianity's way of trying to demonstrate that Christ is the New Lawgiver as Moses was the Old. The New Testament has replaced the Old. The apostles are representative of the Twelve Tribes of Israel; hence the church is the New Israel. The Twelve Tribes of Israel, descended from the twelve sons of Jacob, constitute a masculine concept; hence the disciples had to be men.

Thus there were no women at the Last Supper. But even if ideological reasons did not exist, it is unlikely that women would have been present on that occasion anyway. At public dinners—that is, at those outside the family—in the ancient East the sexes were generally segregated. Men socialized with men and women with women. Nevertheless on the basis of the records we have, we find that Jesus Christ did a very great deal of socializing with women for a man of his place and time.

He loved weddings, banquets, and parties of
all kinds, and so far as we know he freely
John accepted invitations to them, no matter who
2:1–11 the host was or who the guests might be. His
first recorded miracle was to turn water into
Luke wine at a wedding. He attended dinner parties
7:36–50 at the homes of Simon the rich Pharisee, Zac-
cheus the despised tax collector, and with
Mary and Martha, the poor sisters of his good
Luke friend Lazarus. These are only a few that we
15:25 know about. He spoke about "music and

dancing" at a party as if they were the most
natural things in the world. He spoke of the
austerity of John the Baptist without being
Luke judgmental: "For John the Baptist has come
7:33–35 eating no bread and drinking no wine; and you
say, 'He has a demon.' " But at the same time
he said of himself: "The Son of man has come
eating and drinking; and you say, 'Behold, a
glutton and a drunkard, a friend of tax collectors and sinners!' Yet wisdom is justified by
all her children." This last remark seems to
mean that if something seems sensible to you
—that is, justified by "wisdom"—then feel
free to do it. In other words, he never appeared
to be the least bit ascetic or strait-laced in his
approach to people or to life in general. Then
we might ask ourselves why we should not
expect his approach to sexual matters to be
equally as frank and as liberal?

For, on the whole, we find that his attitudes
toward sex were what might be called liberal
for his day—and in some quarters for ours.
John He was completely forgiving of the woman
8:1–11 taken in adultery; the scribes and Pharisees,
a part of the Establishment of his day, were
not. He did not hesitate to associate with
known or suspected harlots, and once said to
Matt. the religious authorities that the despised tax
21:31 collectors and prostitutes would get into
heaven before they did, even though they were
the priests and first citizens of the land. In
the most famous of all his parables he justified
the Prodigal Son, whom the elder brother

Luke 15:30 said had "devoured [his father's] living with harlots." In his conversation with the woman by the well in Samaria he told her that she had had five husbands and that the man she was *John 4:18* living with at the moment was not her husband. She did not dispute the point. Nevertheless, instead of reprimanding her for her alleged immoral behavior, he launched into a discussion of what constitutes true spirituality.

His attitude as to whether women should limit themselves to domesticity or should also cultivate the life of the mind and the spirit is quite clearly revealed in the following little story:

> Now as they went on their way he entered a village; and a woman named Martha received him into her house. And she had a sister called Mary, who sat at the Lord's *Luke 10:38–42* feet and listened to his teaching. But Martha was distracted with much serving; and she went to him and said, "Lord, do you not care that my sister has left me to serve alone?" But the Lord answered her, "Martha, Martha, you are anxious and troubled about many things; one thing is needful. Mary has chosen the good portion, which shall not be taken away from her."

Once a woman tried to pay him the supreme *Luke 11:27–28* compliment by elevating the role of his mother. She said, "Blessed is the womb that bore you and the breasts that you sucked!" But instead of allowing these usual symbols of motherhood to be elevated, he took it as an opportunity to say: "Blessed rather are those who hear the word of God and keep it!"* Thus in these two illustrations, found within the space of a few paragraphs of each other in Luke's Gospel, Jesus puts both domesticity and motherhood in their proper perspectives in relation to other things.

When asked if there would be marriage (and possibly sex) after death, he replied that there was to be no such thing. "For in the resurrection they neither marry nor are given in marriage, but are like angels in heaven." *Matt. 22:30* What he is really affirming here is the completely spiritual, instead of physical, nature of the next world or after-life. Anyway, for him even in this life sexuality was always subordinated to spirituality. Furthermore, whether or not he participated in one or more of the forms of our human sexuality cannot be proven by the Bible. Perhaps it is better that way. Christ can remain what he has always been: a Man for All People.

*For this idea and for general inspiration on this subject, I am indebted to an article by Leonard Swidler, "Jesus Was a Feminist," in *The New York Times*, Dec. 18, 1971, p. 29.

24

LOVE POEMS FROM THE BIBLE

THUS FAR WE have been all too literal in this book. Let us not forget that a tremendous portion of the Bible is poetry, and it should be understood as such. This factor will have not only a great deal to do with our comprehension of the Bible but also with our appreciation of its sheer beauty. Listen again to the verse just quoted at the conclusion of the last chapter, but this time hear it in the Biblical cadence:

For in the resurrection they neither marry
Matt. nor are given in marriage,
22:30 but are like angels in heaven.

Even the prose, when read properly, sounds like poetry. Some passages will sound better to us in the classic English of the *King James Version* (indicated by an asterisk), others in modern translations. We have cited in this book only a few of the prose masterpieces and poetic gems from the Bible. Hopefully we have included such references and material as pertain to our subject. We have not attempted to do anything more.

A small collection of love poems from the Bible concludes our study.

Ruth 1:16–17

ENTREAT ME NOT TO LEAVE THEE*

Entreat me not to leave thee,
  or to return from following after thee;
For whither thou goest I will go,
  and where thou lodgest I will lodge.
Thy people shall be my people,
  and thy God my God.
Where thou diest, will I die,
  and there will I be buried.
The LORD do so to me, and more also,
  if aught but death part thee and me.

Eccl. 3:1–8

FOR EVERYTHING THERE IS A SEASON

For everything there is a season,
and a time for every matter under heaven:

a time to be born, and a time to die;
a time to plant, and a time to pluck up what
  is planted;

a time to kill, and a time to heal;
a time to break down, and a time to build up;
a time to weep, and a time to laugh;
a time to mourn, and a time to dance;

a time to cast away stones, and a time to
  gather stones together;
a time to embrace, and a time to refrain
  from embracing;

a time to seek, and a time to lose;
a time to keep, and a time to cast away;

a time to rend, and a time to sew;
a time to keep silent, and a time to speak;

a time to love, and a time to hate;
a time for war, and a time for peace.

Song 2:10–17

THE SONG OF THE SPRING*

Rise up, my love, my fair one,
  and come away.
For, lo, the winter is past,
  the rain is over and gone.
The flowers appear on the earth,
  the time of the singing of birds is come;
and the voice of the turtle
  is heard in our land.
The fig tree putteth forth her green figs,
  and the vines with the tender grape
  give a good smell.
Arise, my love, my fair one,
  and come away.

O my dove, thou art in the clefts of the rock,
  in the secret places of the stairs;

let me see thy countenance,
  let me hear thy voice;
for sweet is thy voice,
  and thy countenance is comely.
Take us the foxes,
  the little foxes
that spoil the vines;
  for our vines have tender grapes.

My beloved is mine, and I am his;
  he feedeth among the lilies.
Until the day break,
  and the shadows flee away,
turn, my beloved, and be thou like a roe
  or a young hart upon the mountains of
  Bether.

Song 8:6–7

LOVE IS AS STRONG AS DEATH

Set me as a seal upon your heart,
  as a seal upon your arm;
for love is strong as death,
  jealousy is cruel as the grave.
Its flashes are flashes of fire,
  a most vehement flame.
Many waters cannot quench love,
  neither can floods drown it.
If a man offered for love
all the wealth of his house,
  it would be utterly scorned.

I Cor. 13

THE GREATEST OF THESE IS LOVE

If I speak in the tongues of men and of angels, but have not love, I am a noisy gong or a clanging cymbal.

And if I have prophetic powers, and understand all mysteries and all knowledge, and if I have all faith, so as to remove mountains, but have not love, I am nothing.

If I give away all I have, and if I deliver my body to be burned, but have not love, I gain nothing.

Love is patient and kind; love is not jealous or boastful; it is not arrogant or rude.

Love does not insist on its own way; it is not irritable or resentful; it does not rejoice at wrong, but rejoices in the right.

Love never ends; as for prophecies, they will pass away; as for tongues, they will cease; as for knowledge, it will pass away.

For our knowledge is imperfect and our prophecy is imperfect; but when the perfect comes, the imperfect will pass away.

When I was a child, I spoke like a child, I thought like a child, I reasoned like a child; when I became a man, I gave up childish ways.

For now we see in a mirror dimly, but then face to face. Now I know in part; then I shall understand fully, even as I have been fully understood.

So faith, hope, love abide, these three; but the greatest of these is love.

Note: The arrangement of the *King James* selections and I Corinthians 13 are my own.—T. H.

INDEX OF BIBLICAL REFERENCES

GENERAL INDEX

The following, because of frequency of occurrence, are not indexed: male, female, man, woman, husband, and wife.